THE ULTIMATE GUIDE TO GAMING!

GAME ON! 2020

GAME ON! 2020

CREATIVE DIRECTOR
Mark Donald

DIRECTOR OF CONTENT MARKETING
Clare Jonik

EDITOR
Dan Peel

CONTRIBUTORS
Luke Albiges, Stephen Ashby,
David Crookes, Fraser Gilbert,
Andrew Hayward, Darran Jones,
Luke Kemp, Dom Reseigh-Lincoln,
Brittany Vincent, Paul Walker-Emig,
Alan Wen

LEAD DESIGNER
Adam Markiewicz

DESIGNERS
Andy Downes, Stuart Hobbs,
Ali Innes, Tom Parrett, Will Shum,
Katy Stokes, Jordan Travers

PRODUCTION
Sarah Bankes, Alex Burrows,
Kate Marsh, Nikole Robinson

COVER IMAGES
Overwatch © 2019 Blizzard
Entertainment, Inc. All rights
reserved. Overwatch is a trademark
and Blizzard Entertainment is a
trademark and/or registered
trademark of Blizzard Entertainment,
Inc., in the U.S. and/or other countries.
Super Mario Party © 2019 Nintendo.
All rights reserved.
Halo © 2019 Microsoft Corporation.
All Rights Reserved. Microsoft, Halo,
the Halo logo, and 343 Industries are
trademarks of the Microsoft group of
companies.
Apex Legends © 2019 Electronic Arts
Inc. Used with permission.
Bendy and the Ink Machine © 2019
Joey Drew Studios Inc. Bendy, Bendy
and the Ink Machine, The Bendy
characters, images and logos are
trademarks of Joey Drew Studios Inc.
All Rights Reserved.
Roblox © 2019 Roblox Corp. ROBLOX
is a registered mark.
Minecraft © 2019 Microsoft, Inc. All
rights reserved.
Ms. Chalice is © 2019 StudioMDHR
Entertainment Inc. All Rights
Reserved.
Mega Man 11 ©CAPCOM CO., LTD.
2019. All rights reserved.
Shutterstock
Splatoon 2 © 2019 Nintendo.
All rights reserved.

HELLO NEIGHBOR

Find out what secrets your creepy new neighbor is hiding by breaking into and exploring his house—but whatever you do, don't get caught!

STAYING SAFE AND HAVING FUN

Games can be amazing, but it's important that you know how to stay safe when playing online. These ten simple tips will help you to have fun while playing. Follow these and you can have a great time online, while your parents can rest easy in the knowledge that you know how to stay safe.

1 Discuss and agree on rules with your parents regarding how long you can stay online, what websites you can visit on the internet, and what apps and games you can use.

2 Remember to take frequent breaks during gaming sessions.

3 Never give out personal information such as passwords, your real name, phone number, or anything about your parents.

4 Never agree to meet in person with someone you've met online.

5 Tell your parents or a teacher if you come across anything online that makes you feel uncomfortable, upset, or scared.

6 Whenever you're online, be nice to other people and players. Never say or do anything that might hurt someone else's feelings or make them feel sad.

7 Pay attention to age ratings on games. They exist for a reason—to help protect you from any inappropriate content, not to stop you having fun!

8 Don't download or install software or apps to any device, or fill out any forms on the internet, without first checking with the person who owns the device you're using.

9 If you play mobile games outside, be aware of your surroundings at all times, and don't play alone—always have a friend or family member with you.

10 When using streaming services, always check with an adult before changing to a different video or game.

CONTENTS

FEATURES

GAME SERIES

46

THE BEST SWITCH GAMES

94

INSIDER LOOK
OVERWATCH - BENDY - HALO

152

28

104

150

34

158

30

WHAT A YEAR!

And what an exciting time it is in the world of gaming! The Switch continues to go from strength to strength, *Fortnite* finally has a serious challenger to its battle royale throne, esports is bigger than ever, and the future is looking bright, with plenty more for gamers to get excited about in the coming months!

On Nintendo's handheld, we got our creative juices flowing with *Labo*, *Pokémon* made its first appearance on the Switch, and *Super Smash Bros. Ultimate* stunned the gaming world with its fast-paced gameplay and incredible roster of gaming legends. While *Apex Legends* was undoubtedly the biggest surprise of the year, arriving out of nowhere to take the battle royale scene by storm, there was plenty of variety on offer elsewhere—from instant indie classic *Celeste* to the return of the much-loved *Spyro*.

Inside we look back on yet another incredible year for gaming and discover what the future has in store . . .

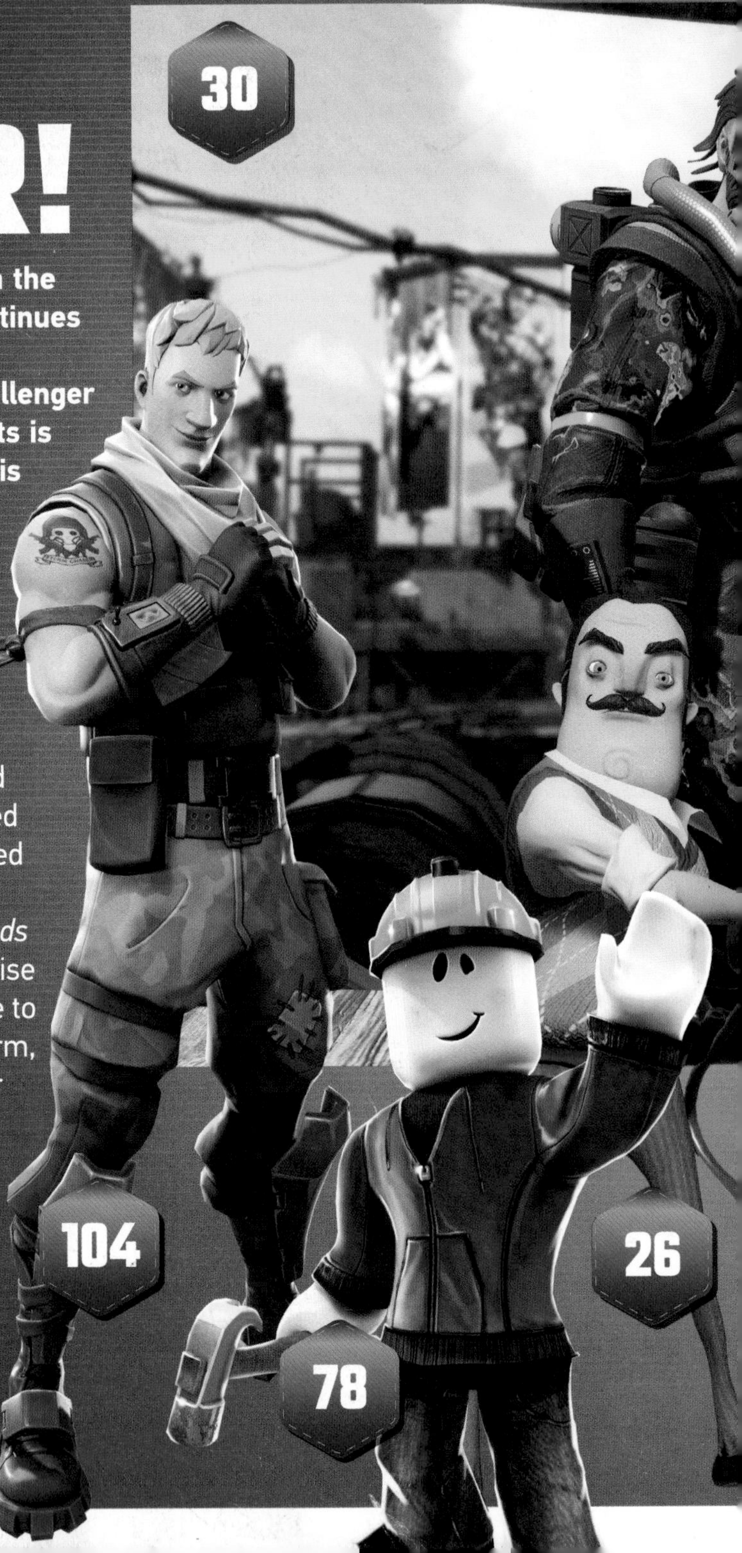

30

104

78

26

94

34

28

150

152

138

50

GREATEST MOMENTS IN GAMING

Check out the biggest and best gaming highlights from an incredible year.

★ ★ ★ ★ ★

LINK'S BATTLES RAGE ON
HYRULE WARRIORS

50 Like so many other Wii U games, *Hyrule Warriors* soared onto the Switch to bring its epic, action-packed battles to even more *Zelda* fans. Produced by the team behind *Dynasty Warriors*, it throws thousands of incredible enemies at you—who you get to beat up with your favorite *Zelda* heroes!

GALAXIES OPEN UP BEFORE US
NO MAN'S SKY

49 *No Man's Sky* first came out on PS4 in 2016, but frequent patches and re-releases on other platforms have completely changed the game since. A procedural universe awaits budding space explorers, with a practically infinite number of possible planets to visit—you even get to name your discoveries!

48

BATTLE GETS ITS GROOVE BACK
WARGROOVE

The *Advance Wars* series was a huge hit on the Game Boy Advance and DS, but Nintendo seems to want to leave it in the past. Enter spiritual successor *Wargroove*—a simple turn-based tactics battle game with beautiful art.

THE HOLE SWALLOWS ALL
DONUT COUNTY

47 Have you ever played a game where the main character is a hole? No? That's what we thought! Still, that's exactly what this quirky little indie title is, presenting simple puzzles where swallowing up objects in the level expands the width of the pit, in turn letting you drop larger objects into it. Surreal, unique, and a whole lot of fun.

THE SOUL STILL BURNS
SOULCALIBUR VI

46 *SoulCalibur* had been absent from the fighting game scene for many years, but now it's back! Most beat 'em ups tend to be based on martial arts, but in *SoulCalibur* each character uses their own unique melee weapon, and some of them are really cool! Can a pair of tiny daggers defeat a giant ax? Find out for yourself!

APE ACTION RETURNS DONKEY KONG COUNTRY: TROPICAL FREEZE

45 *Donkey Kong Country* is one of the most popular 2-D platform series after *Mario* and *Sonic*. Why? Because the games are always, *always* excellent. *Tropical Freeze* was first released to near-unanimous praise on Wii U in 2014, but this Switch upgrade adds in a new character plus various fixes and improvements to get the awesome ape action into the hands of more players than ever before!

THE BUGS BUST LOOSE
EARTH DEFENSE FORCE 5

44 *Earth Defense Force* is one of Japan's strangest gaming exports. Every game pits players against swarms of giant bugs, UFOs, towering robots, and other alien-like creatures, then lets them blast away with crazy weapons in one of the most ridiculous, over-the-top action games out there. Grab a friend and play it co-op for maximum mayhem!

FAST FACT

Earth Defense Force: Iron Rain, announced at TGS 2017, is currently in development and will be the sixth main installment in the series.

NO WORDS ARE NEEDED
CHUCHEL

43 Amanita Design is a master of silent storytelling. Well, not silent, exactly. Here, the excitable fuzzy hero chirps and screeches hilariously but never actually says a word. It's a clever point-and-click-style puzzle game, and every screen features tons of funny interactions that will have you rolling on the floor laughing!

ANIME HEROES ASSEMBLE
JUMP FORCE

42 *Shōnen Jump* is the Japanese manga (comic) in which a lot of the most famous faces in anime were first seen. This new fighting game has an all-star cast, featuring characters from *Dragon Ball Z*, *Naruto*, *One Piece*, *Yu-Gi-Oh!*, *Saint Seiya*, *Bleach*, and many more . . . but who will come out on top?

A PRINCE ROLLS UP
KATAMARI DAMACY REROLL

41 The *Katamari* games date all the way back to the PlayStation 2 era, and *Katamari Damacy Reroll* is a remake of the very first game in the series. It's a weird and wonderful game where you roll up as much random stuff as possible, growing your ball as you do. You can even roll up entire planets if you get big enough!

CARDBOARD EVOLVED
NINTENDO LABO

40 Only Nintendo could find a way to make packaging materials fun! *Labo* kits come as sets of perforated cardboard sheets, with instructions to follow on the Switch's screen. Build your own working piano, handlebar controller, fishing rod, and a whole lot more—or get creative and design something yourself!

RYU KEEPS ON FIGHTING!
STREET FIGHTER V

39 *Street Fighter V*'s roster continues to grow, and the number of characters today is more than double what it was at release! That means you have even more choice when heading into battle, so you can either pick a veteran fighter like Ryu or Guile, or try out the newcomers like Abigail.

EORZEA GOES BIG
FINAL FANTASY XIV: SHADOWBRINGERS

38 MMO masterpiece *Final Fantasy XIV: A Realm Reborn* just got its third major expansion, so now there's even more to do than ever before! New jobs to level up, new dungeons to explore, new craftable items to create, new stories to follow . . . every expansion has been packed with content, and *Shadowbringers* is no exception!

THE DANCE PARTY NEVER ENDS JUST DANCE

37 Sometimes you just have to let the music take control and go wild! *Just Dance* is great fun both as a party game that friends can play together and as a solo game that will help you stay fit and healthy. Strut your stuff to the hottest tunes and see if you've got the moves to turn in a five-star performance!

MARIO PARTIES LIKE IT'S 1999
SUPER MARIO PARTY

36 Some games are just perfect fits for the Switch. *Super Mario Party*, a multiplayer mix of board game and quick mini-games, is one such game, especially since you can pop the Joy-Cons off and have a two-player game anywhere! Add in another pair of controllers for a full four-player party and see who can grab the most stars!

A VR HERO IS BORN ASTRO BOT RESCUE MISSION

35 Move over, Mario. Step aside, Sonic. Platform gaming has a new face and it's . . . this funny little robot? Huh. Just wait until you see the little guy in motion, though. He's adorable, and this VR platformer showcases smart and creative level design at every turn. Rescue all of the little robo-friends, and you can even play with them in a special toybox mode, where they all chase each other around. So cute!

JURASSIC PARK REOPENS
JURASSIC WORLD EVOLUTION

34 Dino fans, your dreams have come true. In *Jurassic World Evolution* you get to take on the role of park manager across famous locations from the movies, building facilities and reviving dinosaurs to create the ultimate prehistoric attraction. Keep an eye on security, though, or the exhibits might turn your guests into dinner!

FAST FACT

Ni no Kuni II arrived seven years after the first game in the series, *Ni no Kuni: Wrath of the White Witch*, was originally released.

THE KITCHEN GETS
BUSIER OVERCOOKED! 2

33 *Overcooked! 2* is a co-op game about running a kitchen, but it doesn't take long for things to get competitive! All it takes is one slipup on the production line and everything can fall apart in hilarious ways, with you and your friends tripping over one another as you try to serve up the customers' meals on time. It's chaotic fun at its best!

A KINGDOM EMERGES
NI NO KUNI II

32 It looks like a cartoon and plays out like a fairy tale, but *Ni no Kuni II* is very much a video game. It's quite a traditional RPG in some senses and plays a little like some of the *Tales* games, only here with an oddball cast of colorful characters that could have been pulled straight from an anime movie.

YOSHI GETS CRAFTY
YOSHI'S CRAFTED WORLD

31 Nintendo's characters seem to have a thing for getting involved with craft materials. First, *Paper Mario*, then *Kirby's Epic Yarn*, and now, fresh from a visit to a woolly world, a certain green dino is getting even more creative in *Yoshi's Crafted World*. Just lovely!

A FRIENDLY AND FUN RPG
UNDERTALE

30 Indie sensation *Undertale* is finally on Switch! If you've never played this stylish and smart RPG in which you can beat the game without even attacking, what are you waiting for? Creator Toby Fox also put out the first chapter of his new game *Deltarune* on PC, Switch, and PS4, so check that out too if you can't get enough of *Undertale*!

THE AGE OF PIRACY RETURNS
SEA OF THIEVES

29 Do what you want 'cos a pirate is free and you are a pirate! Join a crew aboard a galleon or sail the seas solo in a small ship, searching for buried treasure that some scary skeletons don't want you to find! Oh, and other players don't want you to get the booty, either—they may try to steal it for themselves!

AN EIGHT-ARMED DELIGHT
OCTOPATH TRAVELER

28 Classic RPGs like *Final Fantasy VI*, *EarthBound*, and *Breath of Fire* deserve to be celebrated. *Octopath Traveler* does a fantastic job of honoring the memory of these 16-bit gems and it does so with a unique art style that blends 3-D backgrounds and 2-D sprites and an ingenious combat system.

SONIC SPEEDS BACK!
TEAM SONIC RACING

27 Sonic and friends have starred in a number of great racing games, but *Team Sonic Racing* is one of the coolest ones yet! Pick your favorite character, hop into an awesome set of wheels, and work with your allies to secure victory as a team. If you like *Mario Kart*, you're sure to love this, too!

A BOUNTIFUL HARVEST
STARDEW VALLEY

26

Who knew that running a little farm could be so much fun? *Stardew Valley* isn't just about growing crops—you also get to grow friendships with folks from the neighboring village, solve mysteries, and even go on adventures in the nearby dungeon. It's a wonderful game that you can play how you like, and we can't stop playing it!

RACING GETS RIDICULOUS ONRUSH

25

When is a racing game not a racing game? When there's no lap count or timer, that's when. *Onrush* is a team-based car combat game where you score points for your squad by meeting certain objectives. Chase your goal to score for your team and take down rivals to stop them from racking up points for their side!

FAST FACT

Seven of 2018's 25 best-selling games were actually releases that came out in 2017, including *Breath of the Wild* and *Super Mario Odyssey*!

STARLINK BLASTS OFF
STARLINK

24

We've always loved toys-to-life games and *Starlink* is one of the cleverest we've ever seen. Not only do you get to bring your cool space fighter toys into the game, but you can also change up their weaponry by attaching different parts to the figure—which the game will detect and let you use. Genius!

THE MINIS MARCH ON!
NES & SNES MINI

23

There's a lot of love for old consoles, and companies like Nintendo and Sony have been keen to satisfy players looking to relive the good ol' days. The NES and SNES Mini consoles come loaded with a selection of all-time classic games to play, and Sony's addition to the retro family is a tiny version of the original PlayStation, complete with favorites like *Final Fantasy VII* and *Tekken 3*. Great gaming history, so be sure to check them out!

THE HEART OF THE CARDS EVOLVES
DUEL LINKS

22 *Yu-Gi-Oh!* as a card game has grown more complicated with every new mechanic that has been added. But with mobile version, *Duel Links*, you play a simplified version with hand-picked cards that suit the new format. Duels are super quick and easy to play on any touch screen mobile device. It's now time to duel!

GOING BACK IN TIME
WOW CLASSIC

21 Blizzard's hit MMO *World of Warcraft* has been running for 15 years now and some players yearn for the simpler times of the original version of the game. Now they get their wish, thanks to *WoW Classic*, a special version of the online RPG made to feel like it did all those years ago, which is really interesting!

CELEBRATING THE YEAR OF THE DRAGON
SPYRO REIGNITED TRILOGY

20 After the success of the *Crash Bandicoot* remakes, fans were quick to scream that they wanted *Spyro* to get the same treatment. And here we are today, with the *Reignited Trilogy* bringing the original three PlayStation adventures right up to date with beautiful new visuals to go with their timeless gameplay.

WORDS GET POWERFUL
SCRIBBLENAUTS

19 Games that can give your brain a workout are always worth a look, and few games do that better than *Scribblenauts*. The simple puzzles can all be solved in countless different ways—all you do is write something into Maxwell's book and as if by magic, it will just appear in the game! Coming up with crazy solutions in the style can be immensely rewarding.

FAST FACT

The *Scribblenauts* series started life on the DS in 2009, while its latest release, *Scribblenauts Showdown*, is available on Switch, PS4, and Xbox One.

FANTASY LEGENDS UNITE
WORLD OF FINAL FANTASY

18 *World of Final Fantasy* is like a greatest hits package of elements from all across the RPG series. The main characters are all new, but the heroes they meet along the way and the enemies they face are all pulled straight from previous *FF* games. It makes this a charming love letter to the series.

DREAMS COME TRUE DREAMS

17 *LittleBigPlanet* was all about letting players get creative and developer Media Molecule's latest release takes that to the next level. In *Dreams*, you can make just about *anything*, from stories and rides to complex games and art pieces. Even if you don't enjoy creating, it's amazing just to explore the wonderful things other players have made in the game!

WARCRAFT'S HEROES
LIVE ON HEARTHSTONE

16 There's no stopping *Hearthstone* as the biggest digital card game in the world and the expansions keep on coming! The game's simple rules and small decks make it easy to pick up and play. The short battles are perfect for the mobile format. Grab some cards, build a deck, and show the world your skills!

NOT ALL HEROES WEAR CAPES
HOLLOW KNIGHT

15 The gloomy style and creepy crawlies might be a little bit scary, but *Hollow Knight* is an amazing and spooky adventure all the same. It's like a darker version of *Ori*. You can explore some awesome underground complexes and battle big bugs while upgrading your abilities to tunnel even deeper into the mysterious caverns below the ground.

SPORTS STARS STRIKE BACK
FIFA 19/MADDEN NFL 19

14 Fans of just about every sport can get into the action themselves, whether it's the sensational soccer of *FIFA 19* or the fantastic football of *Madden NFL 19*. Cheer on your favorite teams in real life, then fire up the game to play the match for yourself and see how different the outcome could have been. You get to be the superstar!

GOKU'S FINAL FORM IS REVEALED
DRAGON BALL FIGHTERZ

13 *Dragon Ball FighterZ* couldn't look more like the classic anime series if it tried. The developer of the *BlazBlue* and *Guilty Gear* games did an amazing job of bringing Goku and pals to life in this frantic tag-team fighter, and the nonstop explosive action makes it just as much fun to watch as it is to play!

NEW KID ON THE BLOCK
APEX LEGENDS

12 Arriving out of nowhere to threaten *Fortnite*'s gaming dominance, *Apex Legends* is a brilliant free-to-play battle royale shooter set in the *Titanfall* universe. Players must select a unique Legend to play as before teaming up with two other players and going head-to-head with 20 rival squads in a frantic battle to be the last team standing.

FAST FACT

Apex Legends was downloaded over 25 million times in its first week, and it also had over two million concurrent players during its first weekend.

HUNTING SEASON REOPENS
MONSTER HUNTER: WORLD

11 Boss battles are a highlight of most video games, so a game that's based purely on fighting massive monsters must be great, right? Right. *Monster Hunter: World* simplifies the series' usually tricky mechanics to let anyone get in on the awesome action, and expansion *Iceborne* adds even more giant creatures to team up against.

A LEGEND RETURNS
TETRIS EFFECT

10 There's no video game more iconic than *Tetris*. In most versions there's not much to look at aside from the familiar falling blocks. But here, flashy effects and a killer soundtrack add a level of presentation to the classic puzzle game that makes it feel more alive than ever before. It's still the best puzzler ever!

THE FESTIVAL GATES OPEN ONCE MORE FORZA HORIZON 4

09 Race around a superb UK playground all year in the most exciting *Forza* game yet! Pit supercars against fighter jets in special showcase races, team up with other players to complete community goals, and go bumper-to-bumper with rival racers over courses that crisscross the countryside.

POKÉMON GETS GOING
POKÉMON

08 The first *Pokémon* game for Switch is really quite special. It's effectively a reimagining of the original Game Boy games, but streamlined down to just the original 151 monsters, while the usual catching system is replaced with one that feels more like *Pokémon GO*. Will you become a Master Trainer?

A LEGEND COMES CRASHING BACK
CRASH TEAM RACING NITRO-FUELED

07 The *N. Sane Trilogy* remakes of the original *Crash* games were a huge success and we always hoped that *Crash Team Racing* would get the same treatment. And guess what? It has! Slam around crazy courses as everyone's favorite bandicoot and relive one of the greatest PlayStation games ever made!

SQUARE LETS ITS HAIR DOWN
KINGDOM HEARTS III

Tangled, Frozen, Toy Story, Monsters, Inc., and more classic Disney worlds all collide in this stunning action-RPG sequel. It was years in the making and it shows: You can explore the worlds from your favorite Disney movies, and they look and feel exactly like they did at the cinema! Which Disney world do you like best?

NINTENDO SMASHES RECORDS
SUPER SMASH BROS. ULTIMATE

05

Super Smash Bros. has always been an amazing celebration of all things Nintendo. This time, though, it's more than that—it's a huge celebration of gaming in general! Stars from all kinds of games come together to throw down in this fast and furious party fighter, and there are so many characters that you won't know where to start!

THE ROYALE FAMILY
EXPANDS FORTNITE

Fortnite became a global sensation almost overnight. Combining structure building and teamwork skills with epic multiplayer battles against dozens of enemies on the same map, it's a real test of skill but one that anyone can enjoy. That's how it became one of the biggest games on the planet!

MOUNTAINS OF FUN
CELESTE

03

Platform games can be quite difficult, but few are better at training you to beat their most challenging stages than *Celeste.* With just a few simple moves and the occasional gimmick, you can soar past spike-filled levels and over huge pits as you make your way to the top of the mountain, with a lovely story framing the whole climb.

SPIDEY SWINGS INTO
ACTION! SPIDER-MAN

02

The title of "Best Superhero Game" is a hotly contested one. But now, it seems like we have crowned a new comic book king! Swinging around Manhattan in *Marvel's Spider-Man* is amazing fun even on its own, and the flexible combat system lets you embarrass goons with a host of cool moves that only Spidey could pull off. Suit up and get swinging, because superhero games don't come any better than this!

GAMING GETS SWITCHED UP
NINTENDO SWITCH

01 The Switch was a stroke of genius on Nintendo's part. The unique nature of the console has struck a chord with gamers of all ages and the system's library grows broader almost by the day. On top of the amazing original games, returning classics, and essential indie titles, the big draw here is that you cannot only play anywhere, but with anyone—pop off the Joy-Cons and you're ready for multiplayer fun any time, anywhere! It's been years since we've seen such a loyal following for a piece of hardware, but Switch's success has been well deserved. Despite being the underdog in terms of raw power, Nintendo's portable console proved that a single good idea can go a very long way!

FAST FACT

The Switch was the best-selling console in the United States in 2018 after overtaking the PS4 following a strong holiday season.

NINTENDO SWITCH

SUPER SMASH BROS. ULTIMATE

THE DEFINITIVE WAY TO SMASH!

Super Smash Bros. Ultimate definitely lives up to its name—it's the greatest version of Smash out there! With every single character and most of the content from the earlier games, it's a celebration of all the amazing things Nintendo has to offer, and much more! Team up with friends to brawl against Mario, Samus, Link, and all your favorite characters, while unlocking cool Spirits, honing your skills, earning awesome items, and seeing if you have what it takes to become a Smash master. Just about every game you can think of is represented in the very first Smash game on the Nintendo Switch, and this time you can even take it with you on the go.

QUICK TIPS!

DON'T STICK TO ONE MAIN CHARACTER
Success in Smash comes from being versatile, so try and learn a little bit about all the fighters!

CHOOSE THE RIGHT SPIRITS
Spirits are there to be used, so make sure that you equip the best ones for each situation.

DON'T SPAM ATTACKS
Each character comes with a varied set of moves. Learn to chain them together instead of button mashing!

TOP 5 ★★★ FIGHTERS

1 CLOUD
The iconic protagonist of *Final Fantasy VII* swings his massive Buster Sword and deals serious damage—he even brings the Limit Gauge over from the RPG to perform a powerful Final Smash move.

2 KIRBY
Kirby may just be a cute, pink ball, but he is the only fighter left standing at the beginning of *Super Smash Bros. Ultimate*, so he must be doing something right. Copy Abilities, floating, and cuteness—he's got it all!

PIKACHU 3
Everyone's favorite little electric mouse is not to be messed with, and your opponents will quickly find that out. Pikachu can zap enemies, dash around the stage, and zoom about to evade enemy attacks with the best of 'em.

FAST FACT
There are over 1,200 Spirits available in *Super Smash Bros. Ultimate*, and Nintendo will be adding more of them to the game later.

5 LINK
Fresh from rescuing Princess Zelda, Link is a formidable fighter with plenty of ways to fight. He's got his trusty sword and shield, all-round stats, and, well, let's face it—this is the Hero of Time we're talking about!

4 MARTH
If you need an all-round fantastic fighter, Marth is an excellent choice. The swordfighter has range, speed, and power—and he looks cool to boot! A great choice for both newbies and veteran players alike.

ALSO CHECK OUT . . .

SUPER SMASH BROS. FOR Wii U
Check out the last version of *Smash* for classic brawling!

BRAWLHALLA
This free-to-play fighter is fun, satisfying, and challenging for players of all levels.

PLAYSTATION ALL-STARS BATTLE ROYALE
Your favorite PlayStation characters team up for battle.

JAPANESE-ONLY IMPORTS

VikkiKitty is ready to start some serious *Smash* commentating.

VikkiKitty seen here with an adorable plush Kirby character from Nintendo's large stable of characters.

VICTORIA "VIKKIKITTY" PEREZ

Who?
Victoria was one of the first female commentators on the *Super Smash Bros.* competitive scene.

What do you love about *Smash*?
"I love *Smash* because it brings everyone together while incorporating over seventy fighters from a plethora of different games I grew up with as a kid."

How did you first get started playing?
"I began with *Super Smash Melee*. I was an only child for seven years [but] when my sister was born, we used *Melee* and *Brawl* to bond. Relating to your favorite characters helped us have fun, and wanting to be the better player drove the competition with each other."

NICK
This seemingly nerdy guy actually transforms into the superhero Captain Rainbow! This game was never translated into English, so you may never have heard of him.

AYUMI TACHIBANA
Ayumi Tachibana hails from the Japanese-only title *Famicom Tantei Club*, which follows a man with no memories of his past as a detective. Ayumi helps him regain his memories.

STATS

5 games in the *Super Smash Bros.* series

70+ PLAYABLE FIGHTERS TO CHOOSE FROM

DION, MAX, & JACK

Players control this trio in the Japanese-only adventure *Marvelous: Mōhitotsu no Takarajima*. It plays similarly to *The Legend of Zelda: A Link to the Past*.

FAST FACT

Super Smash Bros. Ultimate sold over five million copies in its first week globally, making it the fastest-selling *Smash* title.

SATORU AMATSUBO

The main character of the visual novel *Project Hacker: Kakusei* is a hacker. The game was never released outside of Japan.

800+
MUSIC TRACKS TO LISTEN TO

WANT MORE SMASH?
Head over to pages 200–201.

FAST FACT

The *Hello Neighbor* novels fill in gaps left by the game, such as your character's name—which is Nicky Roth!

HELLO NEIGHBOR
YOU'RE THE BOY NEXT DOOR

He's still your neighbor if he lives across the street, right? But this is one guy you really don't want in your neighborhood. He's done . . . something. A scream, a very securely locked door, and an increasingly weird house combine to create a mystery that it's up to you to solve.

Break into your neighbor's house, explore, and solve puzzles to find out what's going on. Open up new areas to get closer to the truth. But don't get caught! The more the neighbor catches you, the more security cameras, traps, and boarded-up routes you'll find. Will you be able to uncover his secrets?

QUICK TIPS!

HIDE, DON'T SHRIEK
When the neighbor comes close, hide! He won't find you as long as you get into your hiding place unseen.

FINDERS KEEPERS
Did the neighbor spot you just as you got close to an important item? Grab it anyway! You'll still have it after getting caught.

LISTEN UP
Breaking a window will attract the neighbor's attention. This can be used to your advantage, luring him away from a room you want to get inside.

GET TO KNOW THE NEIGHBORHOOD

HERE HE COMES

The neighbor's seen you! Hiding won't work now, so you need to run away and find someplace safe. You can't stop him, but there are ways to slow him down—and ways for him to slow *you* down, too.

MY CLOSET FRIEND

If only you'd made it to the closet without being seen, you could've hidden in there. It's important to remember that you can hide *under* things, too. Even something as simple as closing doors behind you helps you stay hidden.

ENVIRONMENTAL HEALTH

Always pay close attention to your surroundings. If something looks useful—a key, a handle, a magnet—you'll almost definitely need it eventually. If something looks broken or out of place, investigate, although many things are just there for decoration.

FOUR REAL

You can only carry four items at a time, so you'll sometimes need to think carefully about what to take. Even junk can be useful, though—it can be thrown to break a window or knock out a security camera.

ALSO CHECK OUT . . .

HELLO NEIGHBOR: HIDE AND SEEK
The prequel game, telling the story of what happened before.

AMONG THE SLEEP
Play as a two-year-old looking for your mom in this brilliant horror adventure.

CHROMAGUN
Another brain-teasing, first-person game that tests your reactions.

OWEN-B096

LOADOUT: ARC-920 Railgun, MA5D Assault Rifle, M6G Magnum

SERVICE NUMBER: S-B096

BACKGROUND: Reconnaissance and Asset Acquisition

BIRTHWORLD: Eremus (Jericho VII)

HEIGHT: 2.03 m (6'8")

WEIGHT: 107.4 kg (237 lbs)

Spartan Owen volunteered for the SPARTAN-III program shortly after his home world was destroyed by the Covenant. An exceptional candidate, his tenacity and single-minded focus allowed him to grind his way through the punishing training and augmentation cycle to reach the top honors program.

Detached from the rest of his Beta Company comrades for special assignment, he soon applied his lethal talents in the ultimately futile defense of Meridian and scorched-earth holding actions in the Sol System that will never be publicized or known to the wider UNSC.

RAILGUN

ASYMMETRICAL
RECOILLESS CARBINE-920

HAZEL-A302

LOADOUT: M392 DMR, Hydra MLRS, M6G Magnum

SERVICE NUMBER: S-A302

BACKGROUND: Direct Action and Intelligence Collection

BIRTHWORLD: Alluvion

HEIGHT: 1.90 m (6'3")

WEIGHT: 103.9 kg (229 lbs)

An exceptional athlete and student even before recruitment, Hazel's innate physical capabilities were greatly enhanced by Spartan augmentations, and her scholarly abilities bent toward learning the many arts of war.

Her talents led her to several assignments with the Office of Naval Intelligence (ONI), conducting direct action operations against Covenant leaders on occupied planets and destroying critical UNSC information that had fallen into enemy hands.

DMR

M392 DESIGNATED MARKSMAN RIFLE

APEX LEGENDS

BATTLE-ROYALE BRILLIANCE

The latest hit in the battle royale craze, *Apex Legends* is a game that will sound familiar to anyone who has played *Fortnite*. You drop in on a map with your squad at the beginning of the game, scavenge for equipment, and fight with enemy squads to be the last team standing as a circle around the edge of the map gradually closes in. Boasting the slickest and most satisfying shooting in the battle royale genre to date, *Apex Legends* is a real thrill. It's got some great ideas to smooth out some of the more frustrating elements of the genre, too. Attachments automatically attach to any guns they fit when you pick them up, and a fantastic ping system lets you highlight enemies, weapons, and ammo for teammates.

QUICK TIPS!

SCRAMBLE HIGH
Hold jump and your character will scramble up walls and pull themselves up on ledges to get to high places.

SPREAD IT OUT
Think about what your teammates are using. For example, energy ammo is rare, so only one team member should have an energy weapon.

HOLSTER YOUR WEAPON
Holster your weapons and your run speed will be increased.

TOP 5 ★★★

LEGENDS

BLOODHOUND

Bloodhound can track enemy players and use his tactical ability to reveal if there are any around you. While using his ultimate ability, he can see players through smoke, which makes him great to use with Bangalore.

WRAITH

Wraith's void ability allows her to go temporarily invisible, during which she can't be hit. This makes her great for escaping trouble and for getting the drop on unsuspecting enemies by flanking them.

LIFELINE

Lifeline can heal faster than other characters and revive 25% quicker, while putting up a shield, making her great for getting back into the fight before your opponents can heal up. Her ultimate ability brings down a care package with high-tier defensive gear.

BANGALORE

Bangalore's passive speed-boost ability makes her hard to hit in a firefight, and her tactical ability, the smoke launcher, is incredibly useful. You can use it to mask your escape from firefights, close distance on enemy squads, or provide cover while you're reviving.

MIRAGE

Mirage has the ability to send out a single clone to confuse enemies for his tactical and a swarm of clones for his ultimate ability. This is great for revealing enemy positions when they take a shot at your clone.

LOVE APEX LEGENDS?

Get even more on pages 98–99.

ALSO CHECK OUT...

FORTNITE
If you're looking for another battle royale, *Fortnite* is the clear choice.

OVERWATCH
If you like *Apex Legends*' character-based abilities, give *Overwatch* a go.

REALM ROYALE
A battle royale game for fans of fantasy: Swap your gun for a sword!

FAST FACT

Cuphead's incredible visuals are hand-drawn to give them that authentic old-school cartoon style.

CUPHEAD: THE DELICIOUS LAST COURSE

ONE MORE BITE

Cuphead is a run-and-gun platformer with a mind-blowingly brilliant animation style inspired by the cartoons of the 1930s. Thanks to its challenging platforming and amazing, epic bosses, *Cuphead*'s won itself a lot of fans. Building on that success is "The Delicious Last Course" DLC. "The Delicious Last Course" adds a new character, named Ms. Chalice, and is set on a brand-new island. Along with Ms. Chalice's new abilities, there are new weapons, new charms, and, of course, new bosses to defeat. As well as adding another great adventure to the *Cuphead* saga, you can play through the original campaign with Ms. Chalice after getting this DLC.

QUICK TIPS!

CHANGE THE LAYOUT
Cuphead's default controls are a bit tricky, so try a different layout to see if you find it easier.

DASH, DASH, DASH
The Dash is an incredibly important move in *Cuphead* for making difficult jumps, avoiding bosses' attacks, and so much more.

SWITCH UP WEAPONS
Try switching between different weapons until you find the one that suits your style of play.

TOP 5 CUPHEAD BOSSES

2 BEPPI THE CLOWN

This fun fight is against a crazy clown who uses the things you'd find in an amusement park against you—bumper cars, balloons, and so on. He has four different forms to overcome to defeat him.

1 HILDA BERG

This epic boss is one of the most creative in the game. It keeps changing forms, shifting into phases based on constellations like Taurus, Gemini, and so on, always giving you something new to think about.

3 CAGNEY CARNATION

This fight against an evil flower is mainly about jumping around platforms to avoid the boss's attacks. When Cagney sends out dangerous roots, you need to be on the platforms to avoid them.

4 CALA MARIA

You take on this deadly mermaid in a flying fight, first chasing her down across the sea and then through a cave lined with spikes. Watch out for her attack that freezes you in place.

5 RIBBY AND CROAKS

This pair of boxing frogs give you two problems to deal with at once. In their final phase, they turn into a slot machine that spits out different attacks depending on what symbols they land on after a spin.

ALSO CHECK OUT . . .

IKARUGA
Cuphead is inspired by bullet-hell shooters, and this is a great one.

RADIANT SILVERGUN
Battle enemies in this all-action vertical-scrolling game.

TITAN SOULS
This is another fantastic boss-battling video game that's great fun to play.

FAST FACT

The very first version of *Minecraft* was built in just six days in 2009 by its creator, Swedish programmer Markus Persson (known as "Notch").

MINECRAFT
BLOCK-BUILDING SENSATION

There are so many building and construction games out there, but very few of them have had the kind of impact that Mojang's record-breaking title *Minecraft* has. From its earliest days on PC to appearing on practically every console in the world today, the Swedish creative experience has become one of the most recognizable games ever. You can build anything, from the smallest of houses to the biggest of cities. You can work together to create wonderful projects or try to survive the night when the Creepers come out! It's made megastars of YouTubers who play and give you tips while you watch, and it's still one of the biggest draws on Twitch. All you need is your imagination—and lots and lots of blocks!

QUICK TIPS!

POWER OF TORCHES
If you're digging underground in *Minecraft*, put a torch beside you because it can stop any falling sand or gravel from landing on you.

PRESSURE PLATE
Need to store water and lava without it spilling everywhere? Place a lava or water block on a pressure plate and it will stay in place!

GO PEACEFUL
If you want the Survival mode experience without all the angry mobs, try amending the game to Peaceful mode in the settings.

TOP 5 MOBS

CREEPER

The classic *Minecraft* baddie and one of the most iconic characters, this armless, four-legged creature can be a real problem if you're playing in Survival mode. It moves silently and will explode if it gets too close.

1

SKELETON

When night falls, most of the meanest mobs in *Minecraft* come out to play. And that includes the Skeleton, which rises from the ground and attacks you from a distance. Really annoying, but they do drop bones!

2

ENDERMAN

The Enderman is a neutral mob, but if you get on its bad side it will attack you. It can teleport, so keep your eyes peeled for its black-and-purple body. When hostile, they make a noise like a car engine!

3

SPIDER

Spiders are harmless when encountered in the day, but angry when the light drops to a certain level (and in dark caves). They tend to attack in groups, so have a decent set of armor on. Spiders can also see through blocks!

4

ZOMBIE

Another classic *Minecraft* character, the Zombie mob also brings plenty of problems when night falls in Survival mode. They appear in almost any biome in the game. They're slow but can be a problem if a horde attacks!

5

ALSO CHECK OUT ...

ROBLOX
Lets you scan in real-life toys so you can play with cool new outfits.

LEGO WORLDS
Build creations of all shapes and sizes in this LEGO-themed action-adventure game.

FORTNITE
Fortnite's Creative mode lets you build entire maps from scratch.

4 BEST BLOCKS IN MINECRAFT

1 REDSTONE

Perhaps the most useful and creative block in the entire game, Redstone enables you to build working machines and more. It's one of the most versatile materials in *Minecraft*, so look out for it!

△ Inventory ☐ Creative ⊙ Place ⊙ Mine

FAST FACT

What's in a name? *Minecraft* was originally called "Cave Game" before it was changed to "Minecraft: Order of the Stone" (then just *Minecraft*).

3 TORCHES

Torches have so many uses. They can offer you light in dark places or provide a handy means of stopping dirt and sand from hitting you from above.

STATS

17 different platforms and consoles can play *Minecraft*

91 MILLION MONTHLY USERS play *Minecraft*

2 SILVERFISH COBBLESTONE

One of the most useful blocks for building is Cobblestone, which is hard and durable enough to keep hostile mobs out. It's also really good for building roads and sturdy bridges.

4 STRIPPED SPRUCE LOG (WOOD)

Yes, Wood might be boring, but it's the very basis of building, crafting, and surviving in *Minecraft*. It's the material you'll use most early on and it has many different uses.

△ Inventory   □ Creative   ⊙ Place   ⊙ Mine

$$$ **250** MILLION COPIES SOLD SO FAR

WANT MORE MINECRAFT?

Then head on over to pages 74–75.

FAST FACT

During the story, you also play as Spidey's alter ego, Peter Parker, and two other characters, Mary Jane Watson and Miles Morales.

MARVEL'S SPIDER-MAN

DO WHATEVER A SPIDER CAN

Become the friendly neighborhood web slinger in this stunning action-packed open-world adventure. This PS4 exclusive takes us to Spider-Man's universe in an ultra-detailed Manhattan with one of the world's most iconic superheroes in an all-new story.

This is not another origin story, but a chapter where Spider-Man is at his most experienced—fighting crime and ready to put away his longtime nemesis Kingpin. But this is only the beginning for both Spidey and Peter Parker, as tougher supervillains wreak havoc on the city. Peter's also got his problems with his career and personal life to worry about.

Experience Spider-Man, and Peter's worlds colliding in this exciting, expansive urban sandbox—a blockbuster that puts you in control.

QUICK TIPS!

DON'T FORGET TO FOCUS
You'll build up Focus as you fight. You can use this to regain health when things start getting tougher.

UPGRADES ON THE SIDE
You'll earn Skill Points as you level up. Spend them to upgrade your Innovator, Defender, and Webslinger skills.

TAKE PHOTOGRAPHS
You still have your eye for photography from your *Daily Bugle* days, so take some pictures—especially of the iconic New York landmarks.

TOP 5

SPIDEY ABILITIES

1 SWINGING IT

The best thing about Spidey is the swinging, which you get to do straight away. It feels so graceful and effortless as you whoosh through the city and bounce off buildings without losing flow. It's simply amazing.

2 EVASIVE MANEUVERS

Enemies hit hard, but Spidey is quick and nimble. Use your Spidey senses and acrobatic moves to dodge fists and bullets. Jump over or slide under enemies and then make your strike. Those goons won't know what hit 'em.

3 WEBSHOTS

Shoot webs to stun or stick enemies to walls. It's also handy for grabbing objects like trash cans, manhole covers, or car doors—everything is a potential weapon!

4 STEALTHY DOES IT

Spidey can use stealth to get a head start on unsuspecting foes. Hang upside down to scope out enemy movements.

5 SPIDEY OUTFITS

Spidey's got a new, cooler suit in this game, but you can also craft and unlock over 30 different suits. Each is based on designs from the original movies and comics, from the Noir suit to the Scarlet suit (pictured).

ALSO CHECK OUT ...

INJUSTICE 2
DC's superheroes and supervillains duke it out in this fighting game.

LEGO CITY UNDERCOVER
Go undercover to fight crime in this bustling LEGO metropolis.

THE LEGEND OF ZELDA: BREATH OF THE WILD
The most enchanting open-world adventure ever.

TOP GAMING COSPLAYS

SOME OF THE BEST GAMING-INSPIRED COSTUMES AND CREATIONS FROM AROUND THE WORLD

© Madmoon Photography

SKULL KID
by KALDOREI COSPLAY

The Legend of Zelda: Majora's Mask

British cosplayer Kaldorei chose one of the more unusual characters from *The Legend of Zelda: Majora's Mask*, which required her to build the birdlike mask from scratch and create a custom costume. Kaldorei has represented the UK in cosplay competitions, and she even designed the mask to be collapsible so it could fit in her suitcase!

WARSONG COMMANDER
by KALDOREI COSPLAY

Hearthstone

UK-based cosplay expert and professional cosplay competitor Kaldorei has a huge collection of costumes and props she's created from scratch over the years. One of them is the Warsong Commander from the Warcraft universe (last seen in the card game *Hearthstone*). In order to get the full look, Kaldorei created a wig, costume, built an ax and shield, and even covered herself in green face paint!

© Brass Photography

SORA by NIPAH
Kingdom Hearts III

Nipah is an American cosplayer who has been designing and building his own costumes for over eight years. *Kingdom Hearts* is one of his favorite series to cosplay, and he's re-created over 30 characters so far. This design is based on Sora, the main hero from the game, as seen in the recently released *Kingdom Hearts III*.

ANNIE DEAN
Journey

Annie Dean is an artist and cosplayer from Atlanta, Georgia, in the U.S. She chose the game *Journey* as her cosplay inspiration because of its artistry and because the character is such an unusual design. All together, the costume took around a week and a half to make, with many of those days being 12 hours long!

LIGHTNING by QUEEN ADRYA
Final Fantasy XIII

Queen Adrya has been cosplaying for many years and has put together costumes paying tribute to her favorite characters. This cosplay is based on Lightning from *Final Fantasy XIII* and features some impressive custom pieces—including that awesome-looking sword!

SUBNAUTICA

TERROR FROM THE DEEP

Subnautica is an open-world survival game that lets you explore the oceans on an alien planet called 4546B after crash-landing there. By collecting resources, building bases, constructing useful tools, and interacting with the world, you'll work to survive until you can be rescued. There are four modes available, whether you're trying to stay alive in Survival mode, crafting awesome items in Creative mode, taking the ultimate challenge in Hardcore mode, or exploring in Freedom mode. There's plenty to do in this sometimes-spooky underwater game, and you've got to keep an eye on your food, thirst, oxygen, and supply levels at all times. It's meant for seasoned players, but it's a challenge for anyone who loves games.

QUICK TIPS!

UNEQUIP EVERYTHING TO SWIM FASTER
Put everything away for a boost in your swimming speed, which can make a huge difference with exploration.

DON'T FORGET TO READ YOUR PDA!
Check out your PDA for interesting tidbits of story and to advance the plot when you're ready.

A GOOD NIGHT'S SLEEP
Sleep in a bed to advance time to daylight again so you're not stuck exploring in the dark.

UNDER THE SEA

TACKLE SNEAKY PREDATORS

Like in *Minecraft*, the dangerous creatures come out at night in *Subnautica*. Make sure you cruise the safe spots to avoid the predators of the deep who want nothing more than to have you for lunch.

UNRAVEL THE PLANET'S MYSTERY

Try and figure out what caused your vessel's crash while looking around and gathering resources. Something's not quite right, which is pretty obvious, but what is it? The game's bursting with story, and you've got to figure it out.

GO FURTHER THAN THE OCEAN FLOOR

Just because you reach the bottom of the ocean, that's not the end for you. You can go all the way under the sea, as long as you're careful and watch your oxygen. Who knows what you might find?

BUILD UNDERWATER HABITATS

The ocean floor is yours to conquer in *Subnautica*. Create bases that can withstand water pressure and then you can store resources there, park your aquatic vehicles, and return to get more oxygen while exploring the murky depths.

ALSO CHECK OUT . . .

NO MAN'S SKY
Fly through space, discover new planets and species, and much more!

MINECRAFT
Build anything you want—but beware the creatures of the night!

ABZÛ
Go scuba diving and exploring in a vast ocean, taking in the beauty of the reef life.

DESTINY 2: FORSAKEN

GREATNESS EVOLVING

One of the great things about *Destiny 2* is the way it keeps evolving, making tweaks to the game that change it for the better and adding new things to keep it interesting. The *Forsaken* DLC adds some cool new equipment for you to play with, including Cayde-6's hand cannon—the Ace of Spades, a dual-firing rocket launcher—and a bow that can see through walls. It also adds nine new superpowers for you to play with through its new subclasses. There are also cool new locations—the Tangled Shore and the Dreaming City— and new missions for you to enjoy with your friends.

QUICK TIPS!

PICK THE RIGHT SUPER
Think about what you like to do in *Destiny 2*—PvP or PvE—and pick a super to suit.

KNOWLEDGE IS KEY
Even if you only play as one class, learn about the others. Knowing your allies' and enemies' strengths and weaknesses is a big help.

EQUIP NEW ITEMS
If you're new to *Destiny 2* it's important to know that you should always be equipping new gear you find to up your power level.

TOP 5 FORSAKEN SUPERS

1 CHAOS REACH

Chaos Reach lets you fire out a powerful beam of energy to damage any enemies that get in its way. It feels super cool when you time this super perfectly and get massive damage as a reward.

2 THUNDERCRASH

This super pretty much turns you into a human missile. You launch yourself up into the sky, fly through the air, and then crash into the ground or an enemy to unleash area-of-effect damage.

3 BANNER SHIELD

This super throws up a shield with a wall of light, blocking incoming fire for you and your allies. Allies can shoot through it to damage enemies on the other side, which also extends the shield's duration.

5 BLADE BARRAGE

With this super you toss a volley of explosive knives at your opponents. The knives lock on to any targets you can see, so you can use it against one enemy for big damage or spread it out among a group.

4 SPECTRAL BLADES

This super allows you to disappear, sneak up on your enemy, and then reveal yourself with a nasty surprise attack.

ALSO CHECK OUT . . .

MONSTER HUNTER: WORLD
Great if you love doing missions with friends.

OVERWATCH
If PvP is your favorite part of *Destiny 2*, then why not try *Overwatch*.

ANTHEM
This action role-playing game takes a lot of inspiration from the *Destiny* series.

THE BEST SWITCH GAMES

The Switch is a gaming sensation—and while Nintendo's own exclusive games are some of the biggest highlights for the play-anywhere console, the system's success has already attracted more than 1,000 additional games of all stripes. Want to play the best of the best? Here are 20 can't-miss Switch games.

CAPTAIN TOAD: TREASURE TRACKER

Mario's pal gets to shine in this quirky, clever puzzler where you must work through mazelike levels filled with obstacles.

20

CELESTE

Overcome both an enormous mountain climb and your heroine's self-doubt in *Celeste*, a gorgeous indie game for Switch. It's a tricky side-scrolling action game with a great story and charming characters.

19

ARMS

Nintendo's *Arms* is like no fighting game you've ever played: These brawlers have spring-loaded limbs that can launch across the stage to deliver knockout punches. It's a blast with motion controls, too.

17

MARIO + RABBIDS KINGDOM BATTLE

You've never played a *Mario* game quite like this! *Mario + Rabbids Kingdom Battle* combines the Mushroom Kingdom with Ubisoft's goofy, alien Rabbids, concocting a brainy tactical strategy game with a cartoonish touch. It's a bit strange, but also unexpectedly deep.

18

OCTOPATH TRAVELER

Octopath Traveler is one of the Switch's essential role-playing experiences, delivering an epic quest that blends retro RPG elements with modern flourishes, charming presentation, and an absorbing tale of eight different heroes.

16

15

KATAMARI DAMACY REROLL

Who knew that pushing around a big ball of junk could be so much fun? In this oddball gem, you'll roll up an ever-growing heap of items until it's large enough to become a star in the sky.

MARIO TENNIS ACES

Get your swing on in *Mario Tennis Aces*, the latest and greatest entry in Nintendo's long-running sports series. Choose from 20+ familiar *Mario* characters as you slam super-powered shots and try to crush your foes. *Aces* also features a single-player story mode.

14

SONIC MANIA

The blue blur is back in action with *Sonic Mania*, a totally new *Sonic the Hedgehog* adventure that looks and plays exactly like the classic Sega Genesis games from over 25 years ago and is just as fun as the originals.

13

SCORE   0
TIME 1'38"40
RINGS   30

12 DONKEY KONG COUNTRY: TROPICAL FREEZE

The jungle has been frozen over and it's your job to return it to normal. Command the Kong family as you run, leap, and ground pound your way through a series of tough platforming challenges.

MINECRAFT

With *Minecraft* on Switch, you not only get the same brilliant building game that has captivated millions on other platforms, but it also comes with an exclusive Super Mario Mash-Up Pack featuring a unique world and player skins.

11

FORTNITE

With *Fortnite* on Switch, you don't have to be in front of a television or PC monitor to enjoy the complete battle royale experience. It's every bit as captivating on the smaller screen, as you shoot and build your way to survival in each match.

10

9

SUPER MARIO PARTY

The ultimate home multiplayer experience for families and friends lets you battle it out in rapid-fire mini-games across an expansive game board. It even has games that can span two Switch console screens at once!

8

TETRIS 99

You've never played *Tetris* like this before. Take on 98 other players in a competitive game with the aim of being the last player standing. And the best part is, *Tetris 99* is free to play if you subscribe to Nintendo Switch Online.

7

MARIO KART 8 DELUXE

Mario's legendary racing series is better than ever on Switch, with a whopping 48 tracks, a cool anti-gravity racing twist, and a huge cast of drivers to control on both bikes and karts alike.

POKÉMON: LET'S GO

Relive the original *Pokémon* adventure in *Pokémon: Let's Go*, which reimagines the classic Game Boy quest for a brand-new era. With separate Pikachu and Eevee editions, you can pick your favorite and set off across the Kanto region to become the ultimate Pokémon master!

6

DRAGON BALL FIGHTERZ

Dragon Ball FighterZ captures the electrifying spirit of the legendary anime series, with head-to-head fights packed with all of the explosive fireballs and over-the-top attacks that you expect from Goku and Co.

5

FAST FACT

Poké Ball Plus is a one-handed controller that you can use to play *Pokémon: Let's Go*, plus it works with *Pokémon GO* on your smartphone.

SPLATOON 2

Splatoon 2 turns the team-based shooter premise into a battle to paint as much of a level as you can while "splatting" the rival Squid Kids. It's one of the Switch's absolute best online experiences.

4

3

SUPER MARIO ODYSSEY

From a big human city to a world full of cooking-themed sights and creatures, *Super Mario Odyssey* is one of the most boundlessly creative games ever made—and it's also one of the best Switch games around.

THE LEGEND OF ZELDA: BREATH OF THE WILD

Breath of the Wild reimagines the classic *Zelda* adventure, delivering an enormous, open-world Hyrule packed with challenges.

2

1

SUPER SMASH BROS. ULTIMATE

Nintendo has been pitting its most famous heroes against each other for two decades now, but never with the kind of scale seen in the enormous *Super Smash Bros. Ultimate*. It's still a super-accessible multiplayer fighting experience, letting you throw down as Mario, Link, Pikachu, and many others—but with 70+ fighters and a host of unlockable items, you could be playing this one for years to come. And you should!

FAST FACT

You can use the 170 Amiibo smart figurines for benefits in many Switch games, including *Super Smash Bros. Ultimate* and *Super Mario Party*.

NINTENDO LABO
MAKE, PLAY, DISCOVER

Discover *Nintendo Labo*, where making is as fun as playing. The Toy-Cons are made out of sheets of cardboard for you to put together, which work with the Nintendo Switch's incredible Joy-Con technology to create unique experiences.

By making your own Toy-Cons you can also learn how each part of these cool controllers works. It can help you learn to become an engineer or a game creator yourself one day!

Nintendo Labo is currently available as the Variety Kit, the Robot Kit, and the Vehicle Kit, with still more to come. Get creative with stickers or paint, or add new parts to make your Toy-Cons your very own. Let the possibilities unfold!

QUICK TIPS!

FOLDING IS FUN
Follow the interactive videos to build your Toy-Cons. Ask a friend or family member to help, and be sure to take breaks!

LITTLE BIG ADVENTURE
The Vehicle Kit includes an open-world adventure. Use your car, submarine, and plane to complete challenges across 11 different regions.

TINKER AWAY
Experiment in the secret Toy-Con Garage: Invent your own ways to play your Toy-Cons or even build your own!

TOP 5 TOY-CONS

1 ROBOT KIT
Pilot a huge mech robot with just a backpack! Using strings and weights, use your own arms and legs to walk, fly, or even turn yourself into a car to cause as much destruction as possible in a virtual city.

2 CAR
The car has the most gadgets in the Vehicle Kit. Tweaking the levers lets you turn on the radio or wipe the windshield. But you can also use it to throw bombs or cut down trees with a saw!

4 PIANO
Whether you're just learning to play music or just want to make silly cat sounds, this mini piano is perfect to mess around with. There's even a studio mode with more advanced options for the serious music maker.

3 FISHING ROD
The feeling as you pull and reel makes this Toy-Con feel just like you're really fishing! Lower your line and see if you can catch all 14 varieties of fish. Just be careful you don't snap that line!

5 MOTORBIKE
Press the ignition, twist the handle, and you're off like a speed demon! Race against other bikers, challenge yourself to pop the most balloons in the arenas, or you can even design your own courses.

ALSO CHECK OUT ...

MINECRAFT
The most popular game in the world, where you can create anything!

SUPER MARIO MAKER
Build, play, and share your own 2-D *Super Mario* levels.

HUMAN RESOURCE MACHINE
A strange puzzle game that also teaches you programming.

MONSTER HUNTER: WORLD

GOTTA HUNT 'EM ALL!

The long-running series enters a whole new world on the big screen. As a hunter of the Fifth Fleet, you'll explore beautiful environments, from the lush Ancient Forest to the breathtaking Coral Highlands. But beware—they're also full of dangerous wildlife!

Gather your supplies, sharpen your weapon of choice, and eat a hearty meal before going up against fierce monsters like the fire-breathing Anjanath or the electrifying Tobi-Kadachi. Or why not brave the original deadly dragon duo, Rathian and Rathalos?

Take on quests for the Research Commission at Astera, reap rewards from the monsters you slay, and craft even more powerful weapons and armor. Become a more powerful hunter and keep discovering more worlds where even more powerful monsters roam. Adventure awaits!

QUICK TIPS!

DON'T HUNT ALONE
Up to four players can hunt together online. If you're alone, using an SOS flare lets other players join in.

CAT COMPANIONS
Your feline Palicos aren't just adorable, but they're also quite useful—offering you heals and buffs. They're pretty good in a fight, too.

ARMOR UP
Craft tons of weapons and armor from monster parts. Wearing a full armor set unlocks even more unique perks.

RULES OF THE NEW WORLD

MONSTERS NEW AND OLD

There are over 30 large monsters to discover and hunt, including brand-new monsters like the Anjanath and classic monsters like Rathalos. They not only look beautifully detailed, but also have their own unique realistic movements and behaviors.

TURF WARS

You're not just hunting one monster at a time—sometimes two or three might show up at once. They might even fight each other to see who's the biggest and baddest. Use this to your advantage!

HUNTER TRICKS

Your hunter's better equipped than ever. Scoutflies help track monsters, while you can reach new heights with your grappling hook. You can also slide down slopes, which makes it easier to launch yourself in the air to mount a monster!

LIVING, BREATHING ECOSYSTEM

Each of the five major locations are seamless, with their own ecosystem, home to different wildlife and materials. Large monsters hunt smaller monsters for food, while you can also use the environment against them—for example, trapping them in vines.

ALSO CHECK OUT ...

MONSTER HUNTER GENERATIONS ULTIMATE
Over 100 monsters across to hunt—anywhere, anytime.

SHADOW OF THE COLOSSUS
Slay colossi in a forbidden land to save the one you love.

MONSTER HUNTER STORIES
Why not befriend the monsters in this turn-based RPG spin-off?

STARLINK: BATTLE FOR ATLAS
REACH FOR THE STARS

Set in the Atlas star system, you're playing as a band of interstellar pilots on board the mothership Equinox. Suddenly, you're ambushed by the evil forces of the Forgotten Legion. Then your leader is taken hostage before your ship crashes onto a nearby planet . . .

It's up to you to pull everyone together, explore the other planets in the star system, and begin the fightback against the Legion.

And using the optional toys-to-life technology, you can select your pilot, starship, and weapons, slot them together, and bring them into the game in real time. This is an intergalactic space adventure where you can collect new pilots and parts to customize how you play on the fly.

QUICK TIPS!

FORGE ALLEGIANCES
Work with other factions by completing requests as well as building your new team facilities. They'll help you fight against the Legion.

WEAPON ELEMENTS
Most enemies have elemental strengths and weaknesses. Swap in the best weapon parts on your starship for maximum damage!

EQUIP MODIFIERS
Collect modifiers by exploring Atlas, completing quests, or crafting. Slotting them into your weapons will give you an edge in combat.

TOP 5 ACTIVITIES

1 EXPLORE NEW WORLDS

There are seven planets to explore in the *Starlink* system. Each has their own unique life forms and conditions, from the lush and temperate Haven to the freezing Tundria. You can fly to and explore these planets in their entirety seamlessly.

2 SIGNS OF LIFE

Seen some interesting species on a planet? Want to find out more? That's where your ship's scanner comes in. You can also collect samples of the plant life. All will be added to your database.

3 EXPLORE RUINS

You'll find ruins or abandoned bases on your travels. Some might be overrun with enemies, while you can explore further inside others if you can get through the vault doors. You might find that some contain secrets or useful items . . .

4 DOGFIGHTS

You'll encounter a lot of enemies, from the Legion to menacing outlaws. The most epic battles are out in space, from ambushes in the asteroid belt to grand assaults on an enemy base. Remember to do a barrel roll: It'll confuse the enemy—as well as look cool!

5 BEAT BACK THE LEGION

Crush the Legion's reach on each planet—destroy Imp Nests and Extractors, and take down the huge Arch Primes. But the enemy is also intelligent and will fight back in defense—and attack. If you're not careful, they could take over again.

ALSO CHECK OUT . . .

NO MAN'S SKY
There are 18 quintillion planets in the universe to explore. Multiplayer is also supported.

ELITE: DANGEROUS
A deeper and much more serious open-ended space exploration simulator.

STAR FOX 64 3D
The definitive *Star Fox* game, with awesome epic space battles and branching paths.

POKÉMON: LET'S GO, PIKACHU! AND EEVEE!

POKÉMON FOR A NEW GENERATION

Pokémon: Let's Go, Pikachu! and Let's Go, Eevee! are the newest entries in the long-running series and the first *Pokémon* games for the Switch. They take your favorite Pokémon, Gym Leaders, and Trainer talents, then bring them together into a colorful, modern world with plenty to do and see. Whether you grew up a hardcore player or are just getting into the *Pokémon* scene thanks to all the new entries, there's plenty to explore as you choose a partner Pokémon between Pikachu and Eevee and set out on a journey to catch 'em all and become a full-fledged Pokémon Master in the process. For the first time ever, you can also link up with *Pokémon GO* for even more fun!

QUICK TIPS!

DIVERSIFY YOUR POKÉMON TEAM
Make sure you've got a Pokémon team of diverse types so you can combat any enemy Trainer!

TRY TO CATCH 'EM ALL
Don't be picky about which Pokémon you capture. The goal is to catch 'em all, so try to do that!

PACK AN ESCAPE ROPE
Make sure you've always got an Escape Rope handy when exploring—you never know when you might end up needing it!

TOP 5 UPDATES

1 ALL YOUR POKÉMON CAN FOLLOW YOU

Pokémon: Let's Go lets you choose any of your companions to run around alongside you while playing the game. You can even ride on some!

2 EASILY MOVING POKÉMON AROUND

Moving around *Pokémon* used to be a pain—you had to go to a Pokémon Center. Now it's all done with the Pokémon Box! A few button presses and you're done.

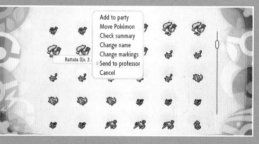

3 SEEING POKÉMON ROAMING WILD

With *Pokémon: Let's Go*, you can see wild Pokémon everywhere you go instead of just in tall grass! Avoid them or engage with them—it's your choice!

4 SECRET TECHNIQUES

The olden days of *Pokémon* meant using HMs like Cut and Flash to get to certain areas. But they took up move spots and weren't always useful. This is no longer necessary with Secret Techniques!

5 INTEGRATION WITH GO!

You can import your Pokémon from the mobile game *Pokémon GO* to your *Let's Go* games for goodies and other bonuses. Now you can pull double duty while going out Pokémon hunting in the real world.

ALSO CHECK OUT . . .

WORLD OF FINAL FANTASY
An RPG full of monsters, magic, and familiar faces!

YO-KAI WATCH
This brilliant RPG series is full of color and fun!

DIGIMON STORY: CYBER SLEUTH
Gather clues and investigate to solve the mystery.

THE ELITE FOUR

Alex poses with Pikachu and Eevee from the *Pokémon: Let's Go, Pikachu!* and *Let's Go, Eevee!* Nintendo Switch games.

Alex and his Squirtle plushie repping the Squirtle Squad.

ALEX "CPTNALEX" BLAKE

Who?

A *Pokémon* superfan of the highest caliber, Alex creates *Pokémon*-related content online as well as a ton of custom Joy-Con and Nintendo Switch artwork. He's 27 years old and grew up with the series.

What do you love about Pokémon?

"It offers a different experience for every player, and there's truly something for everyone. With over 800 different Pokémon, there's a unique favorite for each Trainer. There is no right or wrong way to play."

How did you first start playing?

"I got *Pokémon Blue* for Christmas in 1998. My brother got *Pokémon Red*! That night I remember starting the game in bed and I couldn't even figure out how to get out of the first house. (I was only six!) With some help from my older brother, I was able to start my *Pokémon* journey. Pikachu and I have been adventuring ever since—just like Ash!"

AGATHA

Agatha's spooky Ghost-type Pokémon aren't susceptible to normal physical attacks, so you'll have to tackle her a different way than usual.

STATS

152 Pokémon to capture

23 years since *Pokémon Red* and *Pokémon Blue* first debuted on Game Boy

LANCE

Lance's majestic Dragon-type Pokémon aren't just cute—they're super strong and able to knock out your team with one-hit blows. Be careful when facing him!

EXPERT COMMENT
ROBERT BOWLING
Creative Strategist of *Call of Duty* franchise

Pokémon: Let's Go **brought to life the promise of** *Pokémon* **for me.** For the first time, it allowed me to "travel the land far and wide" to catch 'em all, by allowing players to transfer Pokémon caught while traveling the world and transferring them from *Pokémon GO* on their phone to the GO Park in Fuchsia City! I traveled to Japan in real life. I set out to catch Japanese versions of Charmander, Bulbasaur, and Squirtle. Thanks to this feature, I could transfer these Japanese versions into the game and play with them in all-new ways.

3 MILLION
copies sold during *Pokémon: Let's Go*'s launch week

LORELEI

Lorelei is all about training Ice Pokémon, and she'll be quick to freeze you into submission if you don't bring a strong team of Pokémon to defeat her.

BRUNO

Bruno's a strong Fighting Pokémon Trainer, so it'll be a swift KO for you if you don't have your Pokémon hit the weights!

ESSENTIAL ESPORTS

YOUR GUIDE TO THE AWESOME WORLD OF ESPORTS!

© Helena Kristiansson

Esports is exploding in popularity. Not only are there more competitive games than ever across a range of genres, but there are also more events and tournaments with millions of collective dollars in prizes up for grabs. Even if you don't want to compete, it's amazing to see the world's best players show off their skills and battle it out via online streams and live competitions.

From the Overwatch League to the Pokémon World Championships and plenty more, here's a look at today's biggest esports, the top teams, and how you can set yourself up for esports success.

GRAN TURISMO SPORT
PLAYSTATION 4

Sony's legendary simulation-racing series amplified its esports efforts with *Gran Turismo Sport*, adding online competition that is sanctioned by the Fédération Internationale de l'Automobile. It culminates in a World Final in which only the most cunning and precise driver prevails.

THE ELDER SCROLLS: LEGENDS
PC, MAC, iOS, ANDROID

The Elder Scrolls: Legends translates the beloved open-world role-playing experience into a tense and strategic card battler. It packs in some unique elements—like a multi-lane board, along with runes and prophecy systems—that add further tactical depth to matches.

25

24

23

SUPER SMASH BROS. MELEE
NINTENDO GAMECUBE

It's nearly two decades old, but 2001's *Super Smash Bros. Melee* still commands a dedicated fighting community that hasn't moved on to the newer entries.

22

F1 2018
PLAYSTATION 4, XBOX ONE, PC

The F1 Esports Pro Series is picking up steam, with nearly all official Formula One teams fielding drivers in the competition. Although they race on digital circuits, these drivers wear the same logo and must have the same focus and determination to win.

21

ARENA OF VALOR
iOS, ANDROID

It's played on phones and tablets, but small screens don't limit the strategy and appeal of this complex MOBA, nor its appeal as an esport. *Arena of Valor* is already huge in China and rapidly growing internationally as well.

BEST ESPORTS TEAMS

© Getty/Jeff Vinnick/Stringer

OG DOTA 2

OG had one of the most impressive The International wins to date, taking 2018's TI8 after coming through the open qualifier bracket as a relatively new team. In fact, it was one player's first-ever major event. OG put it all together when it mattered most, beating PSG.LGD to claim the enormous $11.2 million prize.

TEAM LIQUID
MULTIPLE

With more than $25 million earned to date, Team Liquid is the most successful team in esports. Their biggest wins have come in *Dota 2*, including taking The International 7 in 2017, but they have also excelled in *League of Legends*, *Fortnite*, and *Super Smash Bros*.

© Getty/Jeff Vinnick/Stringer

© Robert Paul

LONDON SPITFIRE
OVERWATCH

London Spitfire dominated the first Overwatch League championship by shutting down Philadelphia Fusion in 3-1 and 3-0 sets. Spitfire showcased outstanding team play and offensive dominance in the finals, earning a $1 million bonus and bragging rights.

FAZE CLAN FORTNITE

FaZe Clan has gotten off to a strong lead in *Fortnite*, racking up the highest amount of prize winnings in 2018 on the back of the ultra-skilled Turner "Tfue" Tenney. The organization specializes in shooters and has established itself as the team to beat in Epic's rapidly growing esport.

© Getty/David J. Becker

20 WORLD OF WARCRAFT
PC, MAC

Blizzard's long-running, massively multiplayer RPG has developed two unique esports experiences over time: Arena battles see two teams fight it out for supremacy, while Mythic Dungeon events are essentially team-centric races to be the first to complete certain challenges.

© Carlton Beener

FAST FACT

Dota 2 has awarded the highest amount of prize money by far, with more than $170 million since 2011.

19 MADDEN NFL 19
PLAYSTATION 4, XBOX ONE, PC

One day the Madden Bowl might be as big as the Super Bowl. It's one of several major events in the annual *Madden* esports season, which sees top players representing pro teams and flinging the virtual pigskin to secure the title, cash prize, and bragging rights.

TEKKEN 7
PLAYSTATION 4, XBOX ONE, PC

The King of the Iron Fist tournament returns in *Tekken 7*, seeing combatants square off in thrilling head-to-head battles. This esports scene is rapidly becoming as popular as *Street Fighter V*'s.

18

17

MAGIC: THE GATHERING ARENA PC

Magic: The Gathering established the modern physical collectible card game scene, but with the Magic Pro League now combining traditional play and Arena video game battles, the legend has entered esports in a huge way—with $10 million up for grabs in the first season.

16 HEROES OF THE STORM
PC, MAC

Blizzard's vibrant and fun MOBA brings together heroes from *StarCraft*, *Diablo*, *Overwatch*, and more, and doled out nearly $18 million in esports prizing between 2015–2018. Its Heroes Global Championship (HGC) series ended, however, essentially winding down the esports scene.

SMITE
PLAYSTATION 4, XBOX ONE, PC, NINTENDO SWITCH

This MOBA brings together mythological gods, goddesses, and warriors for 5v5 tactical battles, and the esports scene has thrived thanks to much-hyped World Championship events—one with a $2.6 million prize pool!

15

14

SPLATOON 2
NINTENDO SWITCH

This paint-flinging gem is perfect for high-level competition thanks to 4v4 battles, diverse play modes, and an array of weapon types to pick and combine. The Splatoon 2 World Championship is a blast to watch!

CLASH ROYALE
iOS, ANDROID

Clash Royale is unique as both an esport and mobile game. The *Clash of Clans* spin-off smartly combines card-battling and MOBA elements into tightly paced skirmishes, and those have translated perfectly into esports via the Clash Royale League.

13

STARCRAFT II
PC, MAC

StarCraft was one of the first major esports, and *StarCraft II* continues to thrive after several years thanks to its brainy and ultra-tactical real-time strategy showdowns. It has awarded nearly $30 million to date in prizes.

11

12

© Helena Kristiansson

NBA 2K19
PLAYSTATION 4, XBOX ONE, PC, NINTENDO SWITCH

The NBA 2K League is a major undertaking, with a majority of the real NBA teams fielding an esports squad for weekly 5v5 matches. There's less running involved, but these pros still need to play smart and work as a team.

STREET FIGHTER V
PLAYSTATION 4, PC

The original fighting game legend is still alive and kicking with *Street Fighter V*. It's the major draw of the Capcom Pro Tour and the annual EVO fighting game tournament as top pro players unleash fireballs and uppercuts to dominate the competition.

10

FAST FACT

The Evolution Fighting Series tournament (EVO), held in Las Vegas each summer, is the most-hyped fighting game tournament around.

9

HEARTHSTONE
PC, MAC, iOS, ANDROID

Blizzard's *Warcraft*-inspired *Hearthstone* remains the most popular card-battler in video games. The enticing duels have led to multiple million-dollar championship events, with more than $15 million awarded in prize pools to date.

8

FIFA 19
PLAYSTATION 4, XBOX ONE, PC, NINTENDO SWITCH

The beautiful game is also one of the most popular esports games, with EA Sports' FIFA franchise drawing the world's top digital soccer pros to show their skills on the virtual pitch.

DRAGON BALL FIGHTERZ
PLAYSTATION 4, XBOX ONE, PC, NINTENDO SWITCH

Dragon Ball FighterZ made a huge splash in the fighting-game community, drawing in top pros from other games thanks to its flashy battles and technical, skill-driven combat. It's a breath of fresh air in a scene that has revolved around the same fighting franchises for ages.

POKÉMON
NINTENDO 3DS

Hosted by The Pokémon Company, the official Video Game Championships (VGC) has been going since 2009. Tournaments are held all around the world, with regions being divided into territories and players split into age groups. The top players in each territory and age group are then invited to participate in the Pokémon World Championships.

DOTA 2 PC, MAC

Valve's complex MOBA sets the stage for strategic 5v5 battles for supremacy, and each year *Dota 2* breaks its own record for the highest single-event prize pool for The International championship. The International 8 in 2018 awarded $24.8 million—in one single tournament!

SUPER SMASH BROS. ULTIMATE
NINTENDO SWITCH

Melee still has its ardent fans, but *Super Smash Bros. Ultimate* truly is the most comprehensive and exciting entry to date, packing 70+ fighters and fresh moves into one supersized package. It could be the game to elevate *Smash* into a truly top-tier esport.

FORTNITE
PLAYSTATION 4, XBOX ONE, PC, NINTENDO SWITCH, MAC, iOS, ANDROID

Fortnite is everywhere now and that includes esports. Epic Games has pledged $100 million toward prize pools for the battle royale sensation, and the matches always deliver when the storm eye shrinks and the last few players scramble to be the last one standing.

LEAGUE OF LEGENDS
PC, MAC

Riot Games's hit pulls in huge online crowds—like more than 200 million people watching the World Championship finals at the same time. Between colorful heroes, thrilling battles, and fan-favorite teams, *League of Legends* is one of the biggest esports draws around.

1

OVERWATCH
PLAYSTATION 4, XBOX ONE, PC

It can't match the viewership peak of *League of Legends*, but the Overwatch League is arguably the most ambitious thing going in esports right now. It features 20 international teams battling it out each week during the season and, in 2020, those teams will each establish a home base in places like New York City, London, and Paris and host away teams. It's following the traditional sports model, albeit with the exhilarating 6v6 combat of Blizzard's team-centric shooter. Start saving up for season tickets—maybe your town will get an OWL team next.

GET INTO ESPORTS

NOT SURE WHERE TO START? HERE ARE FIVE TIPS TO HELP YOU TRANSFORM FROM A CASUAL FAN INTO A TOP-TIER AMATEUR ON THE VERGE OF PRO STARDOM

FAST FACT

Most esports events stream live on Twitch, which you can watch free on the web, from a phone or tablet, or from a PlayStation 4 or Xbox One.

1. FOCUS ON ONE GAME

The world's best players spend most of their time focused on a single game. That might sound tedious, but it's key to uncovering every nuance of your competitive strategy and elevating your skills to the top level. You can play other games for fun, of course, but don't try to go pro in everything.

2. PUT IN THE WORK

You might be pretty good at a game, but the truly elite players have invested thousands of hours competing, practicing, experimenting, and honing themselves into well-oiled gaming machines. Becoming the best of the best takes a long, long time. Start putting in the time and effort now.

3. WATCH PROS

Not sure how to improve? Follow what the game's top esports competitors do—and not only in matches. Most esports pro players also stream on Twitch and post YouTube videos, and they might dole out tips or pepper their content with how-tos and explanations. They are where you want to be, so follow their lead.

4. FIND A TEAM

Playing with random online allies is fine up to a point, but you'll never develop high-level strategies and team tactics without a group of like-minded players that you frequently compete with. Look, not everyone wants to go pro—but if you get into a good groove with some other serious players, then it'll help you improve.

5. ENTER COMPETITION

Want to work your way up to the big stage? You have to start somewhere. Look for amateur LAN (local area network) tournaments to enter, whether they're small community gatherings or larger convention-like events. Enter online leagues, too. Every match will help you get better—and get noticed, too.

FAST FACT

You'll find more new mutations the further that you explore. They let you do things like move objects with your mind or even grow crab claws.

BIOMUTANT

MUTATED, KUNG-FU FIGHTING FUN

Take one mutated cat/raccoon creature. Throw in some martial arts. Add special powers and a collection of awesome weapons. What do you get? *Biomutant*. In this post-apocalyptic exploration action-adventure, you control a powered-up rodent as it tries to save the Tree-of-Life, which is being killed by monsters at its roots. It's up to you to gather new mutations, weapons, and abilities and explore the huge world to defeat them. Along the way you'll use mech suits, futuristic balloons, and other weird and wonderful ways to get around, as well as meeting curious characters who can help you out. With a completely customizable character and an endless number of weapons to craft and create, this is the kind of game that lets you make your very own adventures.

QUICK TIPS!

MEET THE TRIBES
Six tribes are scattered across the world, and you can befriend them as you play. It's very useful to have them on your side . . .

LISTEN UP
The game's narrator will talk you through what's going on. Listen out for tips—he knows some secrets that will come in handy.

BUILD WEAPONS
Find a crafting bench and you will be able to add things like electric shock coils—or sludge that will make your enemy sick!

YOUR WILD ADVENTURE

WONDERFUL WORLD
It's long after the human race went extinct. You might find some remnants of the old world around, but this is a wild landscape, far different from today. And with mutated creatures in every direction, you'll be in for some surprises.

CHOOSE YOUR PATH
There are actually three different areas to explore, and they're all huge. This area is the overworld, but you'll also explore the darker underworld and even a miniature solar system as you continue on your adventure.

CUSTOMIZED CREATURE
You can customize your character in all kinds of ways. Choose whether it should be tall or short, thin or fat. Pick its fur color, ear size, and facial shape. All your choices change its stats, but don't forget to make it look cool, too!

MASSIVE MONSTERS
These huge beasts appear around the game world, and beating them is no easy task. At first you might be better watching them from afar and studying their movements so you know their weaknesses when you take them on later.

ALSO CHECK OUT . . .

KINGDOM HEARTS III
The final *Dark Seeker* chapter. Perfect if you love martial arts and battling giant monsters.

THE LEGEND OF ZELDA: BREATH OF THE WILD
A huge open world, an epic adventure . . . this has it all.

MARVEL'S SPIDER-MAN
Nobody does mutated kung-fu quite like your friendly neighborhood Spidey.

FAST FACT

For the first time in its history, *Forza Horizon 4*'s open-world servers can accommodate up to 72 online players.

FORZA HORIZON 4

WELCOME TO BRITAIN

After previously stopping in Colorado, Italy, France, and Australia, the Horizon Festival has finally made its way to Great Britain. This time you'll be cruising around the Scottish city of Edinburgh, passing through the English Lake District, and exploring the beautiful British countryside. The map is more varied than ever due to the introduction of seasons, allowing you to drive in spring, summer, fall, and winter. Each season has a big impact on gameplay, too, so you'll require different cars and tuning setups to deal with icy roads and muddy racetracks. Add a massive selection of vehicles, events, and online modes into the mix, and you'll never want to leave *Horizon 4*'s Britain!

QUICK TIPS!

CUSTOMIZE YOUR AVATAR
You can alter how your avatar looks in various ways, from collecting new clothes to assigning them special victory emotes.

USE SKILL POINTS
By driving stylishly you can earn Skill Points for each car in *Horizon 4*, unlocking an array of unique perks.

TRY FORZATHON LIVE
These co-operative events only appear once every hour on the *Forza Horizon 4* map, so be on the lookout.

TOP 5
★★★

BEAUTY SPOTS

2 GLENFINNAN VIADUCT
This Scottish railway viaduct was opened in 1901 and has become famous in recent years for its use in multiple *Harry Potter* movies. We can't think of a more magical way to get to Hogwarts!

1 DERWENTWATER
This giant body of water can be found on the left-hand side of the map in *Horizon 4*. The Lake District beauty spot isn't just great to look at—it also freezes in winter, allowing you to drive over it!

3 UFFINGTON WHITE HORSE
Use *Horizon 4*'s Photo Mode or a drone to get the best view of the Uffington White Horse, which in real life is located in Oxfordshire, England. The figure is believed to be around 3,000 years old.

4 BAMBURGH CASTLE
If you're looking for Bamburgh Castle, head to *Forza Horizon 4*'s beach area. There you'll find an extravagant, 11th-century structure that you can race around with your friends.

5 SCOTT MONUMENT
You won't be able to miss the Scott Monument in the center of *Horizon 4*'s Edinburgh. The tall, picturesque building is a monument to Scottish author Sir Walter Scott and was opened in 1844.

ALSO CHECK OUT ...

FORZA MOTORSPORT 7
If you'd prefer a more dedicated motorsport game, give this one a try.

F1 2018
Are you the next Lewis Hamilton? In *F1 2018*, you could be!

THE CREW 2
This open-world game features cars, motorcycles, boats, and airplanes.

SEA OF THIEVES

ADVENTURE ON THE OCEAN WAVES

Since *Sea of Thieves* launched in 2018, the ocean waters have worsened! The biggest threat (aside from the sharks that wanted to eat swimmers) were other pirates traveling the salty waves.

But now, thanks to a series of free updates, you've got the Megalodon and the Kraken, two huge beasts wanting to chomp your ship. Skeleton crews man ghostly galleons, and volcanic eruptions can blow you up. The seas are mighty perilous!

Your pirate quests have evolved, too. At pirate outposts you can find traders ready to give you quests for gold, magical skulls, and more. Or why not fight off the hordes at a skeleton fort to claim the booty?

QUICK TIPS!

FIND A CREW
Adventuring on the high seas is better with friends. Jump in a galleon with three pals for maximum fun.

KEEP YOUR BOOTY OUT OF VIEW
When you grab a chest, don't put it in a cabin. Hide it in the crow's nest so it's hard to steal!

MAKE FRIENDS!
Ship ahoy? Play your instrument. Jump up and down. The other crew might want to join you.

TOP 5 ★★★ PIRATE TOOLS

1 MUSKET

When you're fighting skeletons, it's best to keep your distance. Especially when there are a lot of them. That's why a musket is so handy. It's only got five shots, so save them for when you really **need** them.

2 TELESCOPE

Clamber to the top of the crow's nest and whip this out for a better view of your surroundings. If you see a sail on the horizon, you have a choice—either fight the ship, or join its crew on an adventure!

3 MAP

Searching for treasure? You'll need a map. Each one contains an image of an island with an "X" on it. Find the island on your ship's map of the ocean, make your way there, and get digging. "X" marks the spot!

4 SWORD

Your pirate's sword will be the most useful weapon in your inventory. Unlike your guns, this never runs out of ammo. A few swipes will make light work of a skeleton. Be sure to always carry one.

5 INSTRUMENT

Whether you're trying to attract attention and make friends with another crew or you just want to dance a jig, your musical instrument is the way to do it. Hold **down** a button and **you'll** play a suitably pirate-like song!

ALSO CHECK OUT . . .

NO MAN'S SKY
Jump in a ship and explore the whole universe. It's quite an expedition.

FORTNITE: BATTLE ROYALE
Tense, tactical, and much better with friends.

FORZA HORIZON 4
Replace ships with fast and furious cars in this massive open-world racer.

PICTURE THIS!

GET TO KNOW MINECRAFT!

WONDERFUL BIOMES

Minecraft has different kinds of locations, called "biomes." Each biome has its own types of trees and plants, as well as special animals and mobs. Mushrooms like these, for instance, will only grow in certain locations.

FAST FACT

In 2013, a Swedish school introduced *Minecraft* lessons to help students learn about engineering, the environment, and much more!

YOUR AVATAR

Your "avatar" will enable you to do all the building and creative stuff in *Minecraft*. You can either play with your chosen character on-screen or in first-person, where you can only see their hands. You can even pick different skins!

RESOURCE MANAGEMENT

This is your inventory bar. This is a shortcut so you can skip between the resources and materials you need. You can also access your inventory and swap items in and out as required.

ntory ☐ Creative R2 Mine

FOR MORE MINECRAFT MADNESS, ▶

jump to pages 112–113.

BUILD ANYTHING

You can use blocks to build almost anything from scratch. You can build a house, plane, castle, or an entire city if you like. All you need is adequate resources, a decent biome in which to construct it, and lots of imagination.

MOBS, MOBS, MOBS

"Mobs" is a name used for any other living creature in the world of *Minecraft*. It can be friendly creatures such as Cows, Pigs, and Horses, or aggressive creatures such as Wither Skeletons, Creepers, and the Ender Dragon.

TOP 10
YOUTUBERS
PUT DOWN YOUR GAMEPAD AND LEARN FROM OTHERS INSTEAD!

1. ATLANTIC CRAFT

While the team behind Atlantic Craft also have *Fortnite* and *Roblox* channels, this one is aimed at *Minecraft* fans. Featuring a variety of fun video types, such as cool challenges, crazy roleplay and story-style videos, and mods, there's plenty here to keep young gamers entertained and inspired.

2. DAN D

Dan D has only been making videos for just over a year, but he's already developed a core following. Tune in for his jovial commentaries on *Fortnite Battle Royale* and his crazy challenges, and watch as his family gets in on the action. Dan teaches his grandma to play *Fortnite*, goes head-to-head with his mom, and helps his dad get a Victory Royale!

3. STAMPYLONGHEAD

This channel is mainly centered around an orange-and-white cartoon cat called Stampy who explores the world of *Minecraft* from within. Voiced by Joseph Garrett, who also tries his hand at *Fortnite, Ni no Kuni II*, and a bunch of other games, he not only tells stories but suggests fun things to do. He currently has more than nine million subscribers!

4. ETHANGAMER

Young Ethan doesn't claim to be the best gamer in the world. But that's not the point: This kid-friendly channel is all about the sheer joy of playing and discovering new things. Ethan's infectious enthusiasm shines from the screen, introducing viewers to aspects of *Minecraft, Roblox*, and lots of mobile games. Definitely a lot of fun.

5. IT'S ROMELLO

Get up to speed with the *Forza Horizon* series by checking out It's Romello's blistering drive-throughs. Sometimes accompanied by breakneck-speed commentary, the videos include chat and livestreams of *Apex Legends, Minecraft, Pokémon: Let's Go, Pikachu!, Fortnite*, and more, each one bristling with enthusiasm. It's a real blast.

6. THINKNOODLES

With four million subscribers (or "Noodlers"), Thinknoodles presents a friendly face by communicating through Apple iOS's wonderful range of Animoji and Memoji. The YouTuber also gives viewers glimpses of his very cute golden retriever, Kopi, while highlighting the delights of *Minecraft, Roblox, Subnautica, Super Smash Bros. Ultimate*, and a host of other games.

7. GAME MAKER'S TOOLKIT

Older children who want to get under the skin of games will love this channel's fascinating look at what makes them so great. Created by former games journalist Mark Brown, it explores level design and the elements that make up different genres, while discussing just what developers are thinking when they create a stunning in-game feature.

EXPERT COMMENT
THE OLIVER TWINS
Legendary game designers

It's really important to speak passionately and enthusiastically. Viewers want to be entertained, and the pace must be fairly fast, but clear. If we also want people to learn something, we must inspire them to want to know the information by giving the reason for knowing it. While a personality of style, look, and delivery is important, using graphics and sound to add to the overall entertaining experience is, too.

8. ARLO

Arlo is a blue monster who looks a little like *Sesame Street*'s Cookie Monster. The difference is, he devours everything Nintendo-related rather than sugary snacks, forming an appetizing diet of game previews, news, and reviews. It touches upon modern and classic titles while commenting on consoles and gaming trends such as loot boxes. There's also a "Let's Play" channel called Arlo Plays.

9. STACYPLAYS

Mostly about *Minecraft*, as well as animal-themed indie titles, the endlessly positive Stacy uses gameplay to tell compelling stories. A highlight is long-running series "Dogcraft," in which Stacy makes use of the mods Copious Dogs and Doggy Talents.

10. GAMING HISTORIAN

Some adults will tell you that games were better when they were young, but are they telling the truth? Find out for yourself by watching Norman Caruso's YouTube channel, jam-packed with beautifully produced anniversary look-backs at specific 8-bit and 16-bit games, features on old consoles, and lots of juicy info about former companies and developers.

3 WAYS TO BECOME A YOUTUBER
Want to create great videos about games and share them with the world?

ASK YOUR PARENTS' PERMISSION
To open an account and post videos on YouTube, you must be 13 or older, so talk to your parents or guardian: Ask if they will let you upload content via an account closely controlled and monitored by them.

KEEP TO YOUR THEME
Decide how you want to focus your passion for games: Do you want to make "Let's Play" videos or discuss certain parts of games? Don't be afraid to show off your personality—but don't give away any personal details.

HAVE LOTS OF FUN
Be creative with your videos and make use of video-editing software: YouTube has a set of built-in tools, so it's good to start with them. Above all, have fun. You can also restrict your videos to trusted friends and family, or you can use private or unlisted privacy settings.

FAST FACT

Roblox is really popular. In fact, it's so popular that more than 80 million players log in to play it and make their own games every month.

ROBLOX
THE CREATION SENSATION

Roblox is one of those games that might not look like much at first, but beneath those blocky looks and over-the-top colors you'll find a game bursting with potential. It's a multiplayer game where friends can meet up and play almost any kind of genre right there in one app. It even has its own range of toys, many of which enable you to scan them to unlock exclusive costumes and items in digital form. But that's just one side of *Roblox*. The programmers of tomorrow—that's you—can learn to code and build their very own games from scratch. So sit back and get ready to learn about one of the most exciting titles you can play right now . . .

QUICK TIPS!

BUILD WITH ROBLOX STUDIO
If you want to start building your own *Roblox* worlds, you'll need to download Roblox Studio. It's like *Minecraft*, only with the power to code.

FREE TO PLAY
Roblox is 100% free to play, so you can download and play right now. There are things you can spend money on, but remember to ask your parents.

PROGRAM A GAME
You can actually learn to code with *Roblox*. That means you can design your very own game, and even sell it to other players!

TOP 5 REASONS TO PLAY!

2 PLAY WITH YOUR FRIENDS

Roblox isn't just a game, it's also a lot like a social media network as well. That means you can play games in *Roblox* with your friends. Just add them to your friends list and you can hang out even when you're in different houses!

1 LOTS OF GAMES TO PLAY

There are over ten million games to choose from in *Roblox*. Now that's a *lot* of games. You can play them on any platform—including your computer, your tablet, and your Xbox One. You're bound to find some you really love!

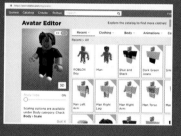

3 CUSTOMIZE YOUR AVATAR

Your *Roblox* character is yours to change, update, and customize to your heart's content. This is all about you, so you can make a character who looks like you, create something totally crazy, or find a mix of the two!

4 BUILD YOUR OWN GAMES

The best thing about *Roblox* is you don't just have to play games, you can make them, too. Whether it's building a simple game based on an idea in your head, or one involving proper coding, *Roblox* has you covered.

5 IT'S FREE TO PLAY!

Anyone can download and play *Roblox*, and you can play most of its games without ever having to spend a penny. You can buy things, such as special games or items, but you'll need your parents' permission first.

ALSO CHECK OUT ...

MINECRAFT
If you want a game creation suite that's all about the bricks, this is it.

LEGO WORLDS
You can build your own brick worlds with the power of LEGO.

FORTNITE
The creation suite in *Fortnite* lets you build your very own maps.

4 BEST ROBLOX GAME TYPES

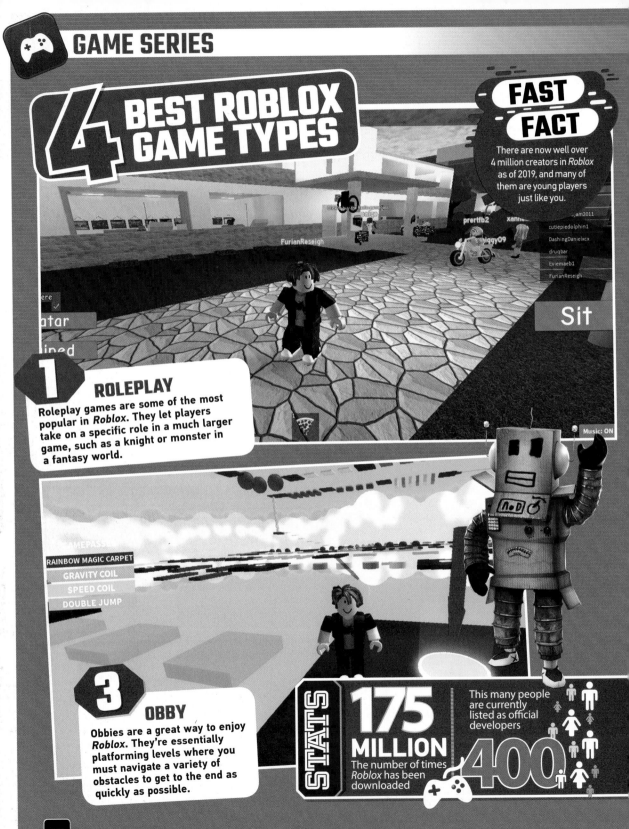

1 ROLEPLAY

Roleplay games are some of the most popular in *Roblox*. They let players take on a specific role in a much larger game, such as a knight or monster in a fantasy world.

3 OBBY

Obbies are a great way to enjoy *Roblox*. They're essentially platforming levels where you must navigate a variety of obstacles to get to the end as quickly as possible.

STATS

175 MILLION
The number of times *Roblox* has been downloaded

This many people are currently listed as official developers

400

18
FOOTBALL MANAGER 2019

Dream of leading your own soccer team to glory? See how far you can get for six in-game months with this free demo of the latest *Football Manager*, then carry your progress to the full game if you wish. What a result.

17

PINBALL FX3

This awesome community-focused, multiplayer pinball game just keeps getting better, and while you have to pay for most of the frequently added tables, there are more than enough freebies to keep you flipping. Not feeling confident? Then practice in the single-player mode.

AIRMECH ARENA

With a nod to *Herzog Zwei* on Sega's classic Genesis console and starring Transformer-like robots, there's no disguising this multiplayer online battle arena game's popularity. It's also available for the PC as *AirMech Strike*.

16
KITTEN SQUAD

Help kittens defeat evil robots to free animals in this teen-rated action-adventure, created on behalf of the animal rights organization PETA. It became the second-best downloaded free-to-play Switch game upon its release.

15

14
FISHING PLANET

There's something fishy about this first-person game—but that's to be expected given that this deeply realistic simulator is based on the gentle pursuit of angling. As long as you have the patience, it's hugely rewarding.

13

BRAWLHALLA

Heavily inspired by *Super Smash Bros.*, *Brawlhalla* is a brilliant 2-D platform fighter that's packed with a bunch of chaotically competitive and casual modes. Your job is to pick a Legend that suits you before making use of their special moves and weapons to battle it out against other players.

FAST FACT

Ubisoft snapped up *Brawlhalla* and introduced Rayman and a new game mode, Kung Foot, when it launched on Switch and Xbox One.

12 MAPLESTORY 2

Bringing together a mishmash of gaming elements from construction to hack 'n' slash, *MapleStory 2* is a cartoonish 3-D sequel to a 2-D side-scrolling MMO and is a lot of fun to play.

11

FALLOUT SHELTER

Fallout Shelter is a cool management sim that tasks you with building a safety Vault packed with food, power, and water. It's important to work out how best to use your resources while preventing bad stuff from happening to your citizens.

POKÉMON QUEST

An immediate hit when it launched on the Nintendo Switch, this action RPG looks similar to *Minecraft* but its unmistakable *Pokémon* vibe pervades throughout as you explore Tumblecube Island in search of loot.

10

9

GEMS OF WAR

Produced by the creators of *Puzzle Quest*, *Gems of War* is a great match-three card battler with puzzle and RPG elements. There's a huge amount of content and a deep gameplay complexity.

DISNEY CROSSY ROAD

This goofy endless take on the 8-bit classic *Frogger* (and a spin-off from *Crossy Road*) involves traversing tracks, roads, and rivers while trying not to get run over.

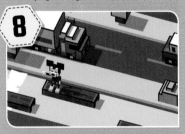

8

7

6

3ON3 FREESTYLE

As its name suggests, this blisteringly paced real-time street basketball match lets you and two friends compete against another sporting trio. Thanks to easy controls, you'll be slam dunking in no time.

CROSSOUT

Hammer a selection of interchangeable parts together and ride away a hero in your new battle machine. Then shoot your way across the post-apocalyptic wastelands of this fine multiplayer vehicle combat game, which now has a brilliant new story-driven adventure mode.

FORZA MOTORSPORT 6: APEX

Racing ahead of *Asphalt* is this free-to-play entry in the *Forza Motorsport* series, created for Microsoft Windows. There are more than 60 cars and six track locations.

5

3

ASPHALT 9: LEGENDS

You may be too young to drive for real, but that shouldn't stop you tearing up the track in a realistic-looking dream automobile. Turn Touchdrive on to play with one hand and just feel that speed.

4

GALAK-Z: VARIANT S

Retro-style 2-D space shooter meets action-RPG: That's pretty much the premise of this progressively difficult, multilevel romp. It makes great use of the Switch, too, with support for HD Rumble and the Pro Controller.

2

ARENA OF VALOR

Having made its console debut on the Nintendo Switch, China's highest grossing iOS and Android game, *Arena of Valor* (a top multiplayer online battle arena game with a roster of 39 heroes and array of PvP gameplay modes), has successfully leveled-up its popularity.

1

FORTNITE BATTLE ROYALE

Once in a while, a video game takes on a life of its own, and that's certainly the case with *Fortnite*'s free-to-play competitive multiplayer mode. After being air-dropped into a destructible online environment, you must compete against 99 other players to become the last person standing. It's not easy, but the beautiful backdrops, silly animations, and scope for strategy make it a real winner.

FAST FACT

Fortnite Battle Royale is continually updated by Epic to keep it feeling fresh, with the map often receiving regular tweaks.

MEGA MAN 11

THE CLASSIC GAME POWERS UP

Mega Man may be over 30 years old, but his games remain as fresh as ever. If you've never played one of Capcom's games, know that the latest *Mega Man* lets you battle a selection of fantastic robot bosses in whatever order you like, so you'll never get stuck while playing. Another cool aspect of *Mega Man 11* is that whenever you defeat a boss, you'll gain access to his special weapon, which you can use against other enemies in the game. But perhaps the best thing about *Mega Man 11* is the excellent new Double Gear system, which enables Mega Man to either slow down time or enhance his attacks. The end result is an incredible action game that really does Capcom's hero proud.

QUICK TIPS!

GRIND YOUR GEARS
Bear in mind that successful use of the Double Gear system is essential if you want to make progress later on in the game.

WATCH AND LEARN
Every robot boss has a pattern. Learn what it is and it will become easy to overcome when you battle it.

LEARN TO EXPERIMENT
Some weapons that you pick up from defeated bosses are undeniably more effective than others. Make sure you experiment with them all to find the best fit.

TOP 5 BOSSES

1 FUSE MAN

Fuse Man's ability to manipulate electricity made him perfect to manage a power plant. Not anymore, however. The robot is another of Dr. Wily's slaves and now uses his incredible speed and devastating electrical powers to battle Mega Man.

2 BOUNCE MAN

This ball-shaped robot used to work as an elastic fitness instructor before Dr. Wily retooled him for combat against Mega Man. Watch out for his many bouncing attacks, and avoid his punches, as they have incredible reach.

3 TORCH MAN

This kindhearted robot originally talked to people about fire safety until he was corrupted by Dr. Wily. He now uses his flaming fist attacks to cause Mega Man no shortage of trouble and can also set himself on fire. Ouch!

4 IMPACT MAN

He might look like a Transformer, but he's actually a cool construction robot who is great at building things. Impact Man is made up of three robot brothers: Kui-ichiro, Kui-jiro, and Kui-saburo. He has a variety of devastating attacks.

5 BLAST MAN

This movie-obsessed robot used to make special effects for films, but now he likes to beat up Mega Man. Bombs are the name of the game with Blast Man, and he'll throw different-sized ones at you. Avoid them all.

ALSO CHECK OUT . . .

SHOVEL KNIGHT
An old-school platformer that looks like the classic NES games of old.

MONSTER BOY AND THE CURSED KINGDOM
An adventure where your hero can transform into animals.

SUPER SMASH BROS. ULTIMATE
Mega Man is a playable hero in this fantastic fighting game.

SUPER MARIO ODYSSEY

JUMP UP, SUPERSTAR!

Bowser's up to no good again and this time he's kidnapped Princess Peach to marry her in the most lavish royal wedding of the century. So it's up to Mario to crash the wedding! But he won't be doing it by just running and jumping on his own. He's got a new partner, Cappy—which gives a crazy new spin to Mario's trademark red cap. By tossing Cappy around, you can capture a variety of enemies and objects, unlocking all kinds of amazing abilities that were never before possible! So get ready for a globe-trotting 3-D platforming journey, as you power up your ship—The Odyssey—(with Power Moons) to explore stunning kingdoms. With hundreds of secrets and challenges, it's Mario's most epic adventure yet!

QUICK TIPS!

USE YOUR MOTION CONTROLS

Shaking the Joy-Con doesn't just throw out Cappy—you'll also be able to make higher jumps.

CAPPY SPIN

If you spin both Joy-Cons from side to side, you'll easily spin Cappy around to hit all nearby enemies.

GET CURIOUS

There are Power Moons hidden everywhere, so if there's any kind of object that stands out in any way, give it a quick poke!

TOP 5 CRAZY CAPTURES

1 HUMANS

Mario leaves the Mushroom Kingdom and explores many new exciting places, including the bustling New Donk City, which looks rather like our own NYC. Everyone's dressed in suits and fedoras, but there's one guy you can take control of!

2 T-REX

Yoshi may be Mario's favorite partner, but there's an even more fearsome dinosaur sleeping in the Cascade Kingdom. Use Cappy to awaken the T-Rex with a mighty roar, and bash through walls and enemies like never before.

3 POKIO

Pokio is a new enemy with a sharp beak—so sharp that it can peck into walls. Capture it and you can use its beak to climb all over levels, all with a simple, satisfying flick of the control stick.

4 HAMMER BRO

Of all the classic enemies that Mario has faced, the Hammer Bro is the deadliest. So it feels great to turn the tables and throw hammers to knock out all your enemies and break blocks.

5 LAVA BUBBLE

If Mario falls into lava, he's going to get seriously burned. But when you capture a lava bubble, you can swim through the hottest things without a worry. Landing on a dry surface changes you back to normal.

ALSO CHECK OUT . . .

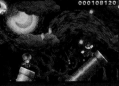

NEW SUPER MARIO BROS. U DELUXE
Classic 2-D Mario platforming for up to four players.

A HAT IN TIME
Help Hat Kid fix her spaceship in this 3-D adventure. Yep, Hat Kid. That's her name.

CAPTAIN TOAD: TREASURE TRACKER
Guide Captain Toad and Toadette through beautiful puzzles.

MEET THE SUPERFAN

NEW FACES

PAULINE

The mayor of New Donk City, and singer of "Jump Up, Superstar." However, Pauline isn't completely new—in fact, she first appeared in Nintendo's 1981 arcade classic *Donkey Kong*.

Mitsugu's *Super Mario* memorabilia was counted by Guinness World Records in 2010. Of course, that hasn't stopped him from adding to the collection.

Mitsugu needs a whole room to store his giant collection, though a lot of it is still at his parents'.

MITSUGU KIKAI

Who?

Mitsugu Kikai, from Tokyo, Japan, holds the Guinness World Record for owning the largest collection of *Super Mario* memorabilia, with over 5,400 individual, unique items. He also writes for video game magazines in Japan including *Nintendo Dream* and *Weekly Famitsu*.

Why?

Mitsugu was born in 1985, the same year the first *Super Mario Bros.* game was released. Ever since his parents first bought him a Super Mario cereal bowl, he's been collecting everything related to the character, from the video games to playing cards to branded tea sets. If there's even the smallest reference to Mario, he's got it!

TOSTARENANS

These skull-shaped creatures are the inhabitants of Tostarena who dress up in ponchos and sombreros. You'll also meet one who gets bitten by the travel bug.

STATS

17
kingdoms
to discover

880
POWER MOONS
to collect

SHIVERIANS

You'll meet these chubby, parka-wearing seal-like creatures in the Snow Kingdom. They also like using their big, round bodies in a competition called the Bound Bowl Grand Prix.

EXPERT COMMENT
TIMPANI

The first speedrunner to complete a 100% damage-less run of *Super Mario Odyssey*

What makes *Super Mario Odyssey* special for me is primarily Mario's movement options. With the addition of Cappy and the abilities he provides, it feels like there is always a different way of approaching any room in the game. One of my favorite ways to practice speedrunning this game is just running around the kingdoms and trying to see if I can make jumps that I've never tried before. There's a sense of satisfaction I get with success from tricks I perform that I don't quite feel with any other game.

GLYDON

Glydon is a lizard with wings, although he can't fly. But as Mario meets him in different kingdoms, he likes gliding from the highest places that he can find.

FAST FACT

The meticulous design and secrets of each kingdom is inspired by a Japanese gardening concept called "hakoniwa," or box garden.

Over **40** **DIFFERENT OUTFITS** for Mario to wear

Ashe is the ambitious and calculating leader of the Deadlock Gang and a respected figure in the criminal underworld.

	NAME: **ELIZABETH CALEDONIA "CALAMITY" ASHE**	AGE: **39**
	OCCUPATION: **THIEF, GANG LEADER**	
	BASE OF OPERATIONS: **DEADLOCK GORGE, ARIZONA, USA**	
DAMAGE	AFFILIATION: **DEADLOCK GANG**	

HERO PROFILE *ASHE*

"MY BUSINESS, MY RULES."

BIOGRAPHY

Born into a wealthy family, Ashe grew up surrounded by privilege. Her parents were highly sought-after business consultants and coaches for powerful CEOs around the world. Though her parents paid little attention to her (mostly leaving her in the care of the family's omnic butler, Bob), they ensured that Ashe had every opportunity to succeed. But a chance meeting with a local ruffian named Jesse McCree, and an impromptu string of crimes committed together opened her eyes to her true calling. The satisfaction of outwitting her targets and the thrill of getting away with it set her on the outlaw path.

Along with the other three founders of the Deadlock Gang, Ashe started to make a name for herself with bigger and more extravagant heists. The Deadlock Gang's rapid rise to prominence put them at odds with the other criminal organizations in the American Southwest; the encounters often became violent. After years of skirmishes and bloodshed, Ashe called the heads of the major groups together.

Ashe saw the potential to grow the influence of all. She used what she'd learned from her parents' business to bring order to these groups. Her proposal was that the gangs could work together (or at least, not work against each other). Her principles: Keep your word, don't work with the law, respect each other's territory, and always punish betrayal.

No longer having to focus her energies on squabbles with the other gangs, Ashe is now writing her name across the American Southwest with a string of audacious heists and operations that has put her at top of the authorities' most-wanted lists and cemented her legacy as an outlaw legend.

ABILITIES:

THE VIPER:
Ashe's semi-automatic rifle fires quick shots, or she can use her aim-down sights for a more damaging, precise shot.

DYNAMITE:
Ashe throws an explosive that detonates after a short delay or immediately when shot. The explosion from Dynamite also lights enemies on fire, dealing damage over time.

COACH GUN:
Ashe blasts enemies in front of her, knocking them away and propelling herself backward for added mobility.

ULTIMATE ABILITY– B.O.B.:
Ashe summons her trusted omnic sidekick, Bob, who charges forward and knocks enemies into the air, then lays down suppressing fire with his arm cannons.

An elite combat medic and ex-Talon operative, Baptiste now uses his skills to help those whose lives have been impacted by war.

	NAME:		AGE:
	JEAN-BAPTISTE AUGUSTIN		36
	OCCUPATION:		
	COMBAT MEDIC		
	BASE OF OPERATIONS:		
	TORTUGA, HAITI [FORMERLY]		
	AFFILIATION:		
SUPPORT	CARIBBEAN COALITION [FORMERLY] , TALON [FORMERLY]		

HERO PROFILE BAPTISTE

"NO DYING ON MY WATCH."

BIOGRAPHY

Jean-Baptiste Augustin was one of the thirty million children orphaned by the Omnic Crisis. With limited opportunities and resources, he enlisted in the military. The Caribbean Coalition, a pan-island force formed in response to the Crisis, became his new home. Guided by his innate desire to help people, Baptiste chose the path of a combat medic and served in an elite branch of the Caribbean Coalition's special ops.

After his service was complete, Baptiste struggled to find a demand for his unique skills. He turned to one of the few opportunities open to him: joining the Talon mercenary group, which was poised to profit off the chaos in the war's aftermath.

For the first time ever, Baptiste had a taste of the good life. Talon's missions were easy and paid well, and he put aside some of his earnings to set up a clinic in his hometown. But slowly, his unit's orders escalated in brutality, expanding into assassinations and operations with civilian casualties. Confronted by his team's actions, Baptiste realized he was perpetuating a cycle of violence like the one that had destroyed his own community. He abandoned Talon, disgusted with what he had done and determined to forge a new path for himself.

But Talon would not let him go. Baptiste knew too much, and they sent operatives after him to silence him. Agent after agent came for him, including Baptiste's former comrades. To stay under the radar, Baptiste drifted from place to place, aiding in humanitarian efforts around the globe. The few Talon members who managed to track him down were never seen again.

Now, Baptiste works toward a better world, healing where he can and fighting when he must. He knows that he cannot undo his past, but making a difference now is what matters.

ABILITIES:

BIOTIC LAUNCHER:
Baptiste's three-round-burst Biotic Launcher rewards accuracy and recoil control with significant damage output. It also doubles as a healing device, lobbing projectiles that heal allies near the point of impact.

REGENERATIVE BURST:
Baptiste activates an intense regenerative burst that heals himself and nearby allies over time.

IMMORTALITY FIELD:
Baptiste uses a device to create a field that prevents allies from dying. However, the generator can be destroyed.

EXO-BOOTS:
By first crouching, Baptiste can jump higher.

ULTIMATE ABILITY–
AMPLIFICATION MATRIX:
Baptiste creates a matrix that doubles the damage and healing effects of friendly projectiles that pass through it.

PICTURE THIS!

BECOME AN APEX LEGEND

95   210   SW   240   2

◇ fraserlaud

◇ adam221994

WATCH THE MAP

Kings Canyon is a compelling locale filled with a wide variety of terrain and plenty of loot to seek out, but be careful—the active play area will gradually close over time and you'll take damage if you're outside of the ring.

ROUND 3 - CLOSING   0:10

FAST FACT

Apex Legends is a spin-off of Respawn Entertainment's *Titanfall* shooter series—but the giant mechs sadly don't drop into this battle royale.

SQUAD UP

Apex Legends is all about team play, and your two allies are key to your survival. You'll need to work together to outflank foes, but also be ready to revive fallen friends and snag their banners to try to respawn them.

adam221994

fraserlaud

USE YOUR ABILITIES

Each Legend has their own unique abilities, including an ultimate that can be hugely powerful—such as calling in a mortar strike or creating portals that you can zip through. Be sure to save yours for when it'll help your squad the most.

Ted_Breakfast 🔊

12

L1

285   300   NW   330   345   N   15

DON'T STOP!

Staying in any one place for too long is an invitation for enemies to take you out. Luckily, *Apex Legends* provides many ways to keep moving through the world, whether it's by zipline, climbing walls, or gleefully sliding down slopes.

GET COLORFUL

Apex Legends has loads and loads of unlockable customization items, including weapon skins, vibrant Legend costumes, and flashy finishing moves. You can buy some of this stuff, but thankfully, you'll also get plenty of free gear just by playing.

SQUADS LEFT

WANT TO BE THE BEST? ▶

Head to pages 154–155 to find out how.

44

○ 25

DEVOTION   △ PEACEKEEPER

FAST FACT

Including downloadable content, plus Expansion packs, Game packs, and Stuff packs, *The Sims 4* has over 30 add-ons!

THE SIMS 4

LIVING IT UP

The Sims is a life simulator where you can create your own character, build their house, and manage their life—making friends, getting married, getting a job to earn cash, and so on. Since the game's release, developer Maxis has continued to add new features and release new content to give you new ways to play with your Sims, their houses, and their communities. This includes the addition of swimming pools and basements, new careers such as doctor and detective, the ability to join clubs with Sims that share similar interests, new neighborhoods, pets, and much, much more. That means there's now a crazy amount of options for you to enjoy in a life simulator that just keeps on growing.

QUICK TIPS!

NEW TUNES
On PC, you can copy MP3 files into "The Sims4\Custom Music" folder to hear your own music via the in-game radio.

DON'T OVERDO IT
You can't always satisfy all your Sims' needs in one day. Instead, plan your week to address their different needs.

FREE CASH
On PC, press Ctrl + Shift + C to open the Cheat Console and then type "motherlode" to get 50,000 simoleons.

TOP 5 ★★★ ADD-ONS

1 CITY LIVING

City Living adds a whole new world called San Myshuno, featuring penthouses, a karaoke bar, a park, an art center, and apartments. It adds a bunch of new festivals for you to enjoy, the new singing skill, and new careers for you to explore.

2 CATS AND DOGS

Who doesn't want a cute cat or dog as part of their Sims family? This expansion gives you the opportunity to do just that as well as adding the ability to create your own veterinary practice and start a career as a vet.

3 VAMPIRES

Sometimes it's fun to move away from the realism that *The Sims* offers and have some fun. The Vampires pack is perfect for that, allowing you to create vampires with different powers and live in a new vampire-themed neighborhood called Forgotten Hollow.

GET TO WORK 4

This pack includes a new neighborhood, Magnolia Promenade, where you can go shopping; three new playable careers; the ability to build your own store; new skills; and even an alien neighborhood with playable alien Sims.

5 PARENTHOOD

This content pack adds parenting: new character traits, sibling rivalries, the ability to set curfews, and new interactive objects, including school projects and a family bulletin board.

ALSO CHECK OUT...

CITIES: SKYLINES
If you love building, this city simulation is perfect.

ANIMAL CROSSING: POCKET CAMP
A cute life sim to play on the go on mobile.

HATOFUL BOYFRIEND
If you like romance in *The Sims*, how about this dating game?

TOP 10

COLLECTIBLES
THE OPTIONAL ITEMS THAT MAKE GAMES EVEN MORE FUN

1 PIRATE LEGEND OUTFIT
Sea of Thieves

Becoming a Pirate Legend in *Sea of Thieves* isn't easy, but the rewards are awesome. You'll have to reach level 40 with each of the guilds, then solve a riddle that takes you to the legendary hideout. Once you're there you'll get an incredible new outfit to show off to your friends as you sail the high seas. Y'arrr!

2 BACKPACKS Spider-Man

There are plenty of reasons to grab the backpacks that Peter Parker left scattered around New York in *Spider-Man*. Not only will you get a cool item that comic-book fans will recognize, you'll also get a Backpack Token that can be used to spend on upgrades. Find all 55 backpacks and you'll get a special suit.

3 CHARACTERS Super Smash Bros. Ultimate

With over 70 characters to unlock in *Ultimate*, collecting every last one is a big part of the game. And, because each one is unique, every time you unlock someone new you get to try a whole new way to play. Collecting them all will take work and a few trips through the game's Classic Mode—then you can pick a favorite.

4 SOUVENIRS
Super Mario Odyssey

Some of the best collectibles in games aren't about new upgrades or extra abilities. Sometimes they're just about celebrating your achievements, which is why the Souvenirs in Mario's latest adventure are so cool. You can buy one from each world you visit, and they'll be added to your ship.

5 ARMOR OF THE WILD

The Legend of Zelda: Breath of the Wild

A special outfit that matches the famous Link look. You'll have to beat 120 shrines to get it, but you'll not only look like the hero of old—you'll also have great defense stats.

6 SHIPS

Starlink: Battle for Atlas

Your ship is completely customizable—you can add different weapons, change the pilots, or even swap the whole ship as you play. You can collect all of these in the real world, if you want, because the smart toys can be attached to a controller to appear on-screen.

7 POKÉMON

Pokémon: Let's Go

In *Let's Go, Pikachu!* and *Let's Go, Eevee!*, you'll run into wild Pokémon all the time as you explore the world—and when you do, you should catch them! Completing your Pokédex is a big challenge, as there are 151 to find. Get them all and you'll be a true Pokémon master.

8 CARS

Forza Horizon 4

As you explore a reimagined version of the UK in some of the coolest cars in the world, you'll earn in-game money. Save up enough and you can unlock new cars and add them to your garage. Collecting as many awesome vehicles as you can and driving them across the country at high speed is all part of the fun.

9 DANCES

Fortnite

Everyone knows that *Fortnite* isn't just about fighting for survival in a huge battle royale. It's also about celebrating with super-cool dance moves. There are dozens to choose from and collecting the best ones means that you'll always be ready to bust a move when the moment comes. We still love the floss, even if it is kind of old now.

EXPERT COMMENT
STEPHEN ASHBY
Former editor of *Official Xbox Magazine*

Stardew Valley **has a ton of cool collectibles to find.** In fact, one part of the game is filling up the town's museum with old artifacts that you find as you play. You might dig them up, discover them in the mines, or even hook them with your fishing rod! I've still got a lot to find, but discovering things about the world by unearthing these old items is a real joy.

10 RED BRICKS

LEGO DC Super-Villains

The Red Bricks in LEGO games aren't just a challenging collectible for you to find and gather. They also help you by giving you extra abilities or fun new skills. For example, some Red Bricks multiply the number of studs you collect, so you can unlock characters faster. Others make your footprints look like paint splatters or make your punches explode with confetti!

3 WAYS TO FIND HIDDEN COLLECTIBLES

Our tips on how to dig out the secret items and complete your collection.

REVIST AREAS
As you get more abilities and powers in the game, try going back to earlier levels and using them to see if there is anything new or hidden that you missed the first time around.

LOOK EVERYWHERE
Collectibles are often hidden in hard-to-reach places, or down paths that lead to a dead end. Don't ignore doors or areas because they're off the beaten track—they will often hold secrets.

GET HELP
If you've only got a few collectibles left in a game and really want to 100% complete it, why not get some help? Looking for a walkthrough online, watching videos of people playing, or asking a friend for a tip is a great idea.

FAST FACT

Fortnite was first unveiled in 2011, but the original *Save the World* game didn't release to the public until July 2017.

FORTNITE
PREPARE FOR BATTLE

One hundred players are dropped onto an island, forced to scavenge for supplies, and the last one standing is the winner. The game gets even better when you start adding skins for your character, collecting hilarious emotes, and sampling its excellent Limited Time Modes. *Fortnite* remains best known for its *Battle Royale* component, but there's plenty to enjoy away from the battlefield, too, including a brilliant Creative mode and an exhaustive *Save the World* campaign. It's no surprise that Epic Games's superb title remains one of the most popular games in the world, with masses of players logging in on a daily basis.

QUICK TIPS!

ACCOUNT SAFETY
It's important to keep your account safe with two-factor authentication. Activate it at **epicgames.com**.

CHANGE THE CONTROLS
You can customize *Fortnite*'s controls in multiple ways via the settings menu, altering everything from controller presets to auto assistance.

CROSS-PLATFORM
Fortnite Battle Royale supports cross-platform play, allowing you to compete alongside your friends on supported console, PC, and mobile devices.

TOP 5 SKINS

★★★

BEEF BOSS **1**

Everyone loves the Durr Burger! This hilarious skin is part of the Durr Burger set and can be purchased alongside items such as a fast food–inspired Back Bling and condiment-filled glider. You'll occasionally find it in the Item Shop.

3 LUCHA

Both the Masked Fury (male) and Dynamo (female) skins are part of the Lucha set, allowing players to role-play as an epic Mexican luchador. You'll find them for 1,200 V-Bucks when made available in the Item Shop.

2 MAGNUS

This menacing, Viking-style skin is a great costume for striking fear into your enemies. First introduced in Season 5, it isn't available all that regularly, but can be obtained alongside four additional items in the Norse set.

4 YEE-HAW!

You may already own the male version of this skin, which was featured in the Season 6 Battle Pass. If not, don't fear—the Llama-riding outfit is sometimes available in a female version from the Item Shop, entitled "Yee-Haw!"

VALKYRIE **5**

Again, the male version of this skin (Ragnarok) was made available in a previous Battle Pass. That one was obtained at Tier 100, but we think this female version is even better. Get it for 2,000 V-Bucks in the Item Shop.

ALSO CHECK OUT . . .

REALM ROYALE
This game features various classes and crafting options.

MINECRAFT
If you like *Fortnite*'s Creative mode, you'll love *Minecraft*.

ROBLOX
You can play practically anything in *Roblox*, including battle royale.

MEET THE SUPERFAN

BrickinNick's Loot Llama is made up of several thousand LEGO pieces. The side panels can even be opened to access the precious loot inside!

BRICKINNICK

Who?

Nick is a content creator who regularly streams his incredible LEGO builds live on Twitch. He's made use of thousands of LEGO pieces to craft a whole range of *Fortnite*-inspired creations, including a Brite Bag and the epic Rainbow Smash Pickaxe, as seen above.

Why?

Nick has been passionate about building with LEGO his entire life and took an interest in *Fortnite* soon after its *Battle Royale* mode first launched in September 2017. After watching various friends playing the game, he quickly grew fond of its exciting gameplay and unique graphics, characters, and items.

4 BATTLE PASS TIPS

1

SAVE YOUR V-BUCKS

If you collect and save at least 950 V-Bucks per season via the Battle Pass, you'll be able to afford next season's Battle Pass without spending any real money.

2

USE LTMS TO COMPLETE OBJECTIVES

Limited Time Modes are a great way of completing challenges. Try to wait for the modes that include respawning, as these allow more room for error.

STATS

7 playable platforms

200 MILLION registered players

10 WEEKS OF CHALLENGES per season

3
PLAY TOGETHER FOR XP BOOSTS

The Battle Pass typically includes XP boosts for playing with friends, allowing you to level up more quickly when playing in a group. Take advantage of this when you can.

4
COMPLETE YOUR DAILY CHALLENGES

Daily Challenges not only serve as a way of increasing your Battle Pass tier, but they also unlock rewards for your inventory on occasion.

EXPERT COMMENT
ERIC WILLIAMSON
Design Lead, *Fortnite Battle Royale*

"When we first launched *Battle Royale* we knew we had work to do. We had an idea of where the game would go but [we] wanted to stay open—not only listening to feedback, but actually being able to act on it," Eric told *GamesTM* magazine in 2018. "We think of the game as a canvas and a set of tools for players to use and have fun with. It's really cool to see the things they come up with—whether it's rocket riding or a unique way to use building."

FAST FACT

If you don't like your daily challenge, you can change it. Just hit "Inspect Challenges" in the lobby, followed by "Replace Quest."

LOVE FORTNITE?
Jump to pages 156–157 for more!

FAST FACT

Hidden on Celeste Mountain are secret cassette tapes which can unlock harder "B-Side" versions of the levels. Try and pick some up for retro fun!

CELESTE
THE SUMMIT OF GAMING GREATNESS

The goal of *Celeste* is to guide the game's star, Madeline, to the top of the perilous Celeste Mountain. What follows is a series of tough platforming challenges featuring moving platforms, deadly spikes, and a whole host of other hazards and obstacles to overcome. Madeline is up to the task thanks to a cool mid-air dash ability that can be recharged mid-flight when you hit special crystals, effectively allowing you to fly through levels in the game's trickier sections. Many of the game's challenges seems impossibly difficult at first. However, quick restarts encourage you to keep trying and, if you stick with it, you will go further and further until you eventually beat them. When you do, it feels amazing! The satisfaction will keep you going until you hit the peak.

QUICK TIPS!

FAILING IS FINE
You're supposed to fail a lot in *Celeste*, so don't get too frustrated! Take your time and focus on just making small improvements rather than expecting huge leaps forward.

TRY THE D-PAD
Give the D-pad a go—you might find it suits the game's eight-directional movement a bit better than the analog stick.

USE ASSISTS
If you're not enjoying the game's difficulty, head into the option menu and turn on some assists.

TOP 5 ★★★ COOL FEATURES

2 THE STRAWBERRIES

If you love *Celeste*'s tough platforming, then you'll want to keep an eye out for the strawberries that are placed around the game's world. They are very hard to get, but thankfully, completely optional if you'd prefer to leave them.

1 THE MOUNTAIN

The design of the mountain's platforming levels is amazing. There are always cool new ideas being introduced to keep the game interesting, and it manages to be challenging without being off-puttingly difficult, in part thanks to some optional assists to make it easier.

3 MADELINE

Madeline feels great to control as you leap, climb, and dash your way through the world. She's also a kind, friendly, and likable character, which makes her a joy to experience the game's story with.

4 THE STORY

As well as being a great game, *Celeste* tells an inspiring story about Madeline's struggle with her bad side, known as Badeline, and how she must overcome it to achieve her goals.

5 THE CHARACTERS

There is a cast of fun and eccentric characters for you to meet as you make your way to the peak of Mount Celeste, including Granny, the hotel concierge Mr. Oshiro, and the friendly Theo.

ALSO CHECK OUT . . .

CROAKER: HEY SHOVEL KNIGHT, I KNOW THINGS ARE TOUGH, BUT DON'T THROW IN THE TROWEL!

SHOVEL KNIGHT: TREASURE TROVE
Tough pixel-art platformer.

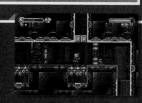

TOWERFALL
A fun multiplayer title made by the developer behind *Celeste*.

ICONOCLASTS
Old school–inspired platformer with challenge and humor.

TRIALS RISING

THE RIDE OF YOUR LIFE

Trials is going back to basics in the latest entry in the back-flipping, wheelie-popping series. In *Rising*, you'll visit some of the world's most famous landmarks. That means revving up the side of Mount Everest, zooming through Yellowstone National Park, and pulling triple backflips off the Eiffel Tower.

In case you hadn't realized, this motorcycle racer isn't *entirely* realistic. In fact, one of the biggest draws of *Trials* is failing to complete courses due to ridiculous mistakes or outrageous obstacles. Will you be knocked off your bike by the huge wrecking ball? Or perhaps you'll misjudge a backflip and land upside down. Whatever happens, don't worry—a quick button press and you'll be back on your bike, ready to try again.

QUICK TIPS!

FLIP CAREFULLY
Don't attempt to pull off a triple backflip on every single jump you do. It's way too risky and might even end in a crash.

RETRY
Don't worry about hitting retry if it doesn't go well—practice makes perfect, remember.

LEARN THE BIKE
There are several bikes to choose from and they are all totally different. Try using each one until you have mastered it.

TOP 5 GAME MODES

1 SINGLE PLAYER
Once you've beaten the course and set a great time, why not revisit it and try to beat some of the game's other challenges? Each stage has a few to try and they're all crazy. Give them a go!

2 ONLINE MULTIPLAYER
Join your friends online and you will face off on an enormous course with room for up to eight racers. You can see how your competitors are doing as you race, so you'll know just how close you are to actually winning.

3 TANDEM
This new mode puts two racers on the same bike, as the name suggests. Each player will have control over half of the bike's balance and half of the bike's acceleration. You'll need to work together if you want to avoid crashing.

4 TIME TRIAL
In this mode you'll see other players on the course as you race. Don't worry—you can't crash into them. It's just a useful way to see your friends' times, so you know whether or not you're on track to beat them.

5 LOCAL MULTIPLAYER
Get comfy with friends in front of the TV as you race on the same console. If you're playing multiplayer, expect lots of laughter, excited shouting, and a tense final few seconds.

ALSO CHECK OUT...

TRACKMANIA TURBO
Drive along walls, through loops, and more in this 3-D racer.

ONRUSH
Crashes, jumps, and boosts are all part of this rally title, so be prepared!

TRIALS FUSION
The previous game in the *Trials* series was a more futuristic take.

BUILD A SECRET LAIR IN MINECRAFT

CREATE YOUR VERY OWN SECRET HIDEAWAY IN 10 EASY STEPS

FIND A HILL

1 In order to build a secret lair or base, it's much easier and faster to find something to build your base within. Use a biome such as Forests, Mesa, or Extreme Hills so you've got lots of choices when it comes to locations. Look for something that's nearby and is around four or five blocks high as your starting point.

START DIGGING YOUR BASE

2 Now that you've picked a location, start digging your entrance. This can vary in size, but we've gone for an entrance corridor that's one block wide and two blocks high. That makes it big enough for your avatar, but small enough to be hidden to anyone else or hostile mobs. Dig forward as far as you'd like.

BEST BIOMES IN MINECRAFT
Get to know the best locations and settings in the world of mining and crafting.

PLAINS
One of the most commonly used biomes in all of *Minecraft*, the Plains are designed to be flat and open, with lots of grass and the occasional tree. Lots of different mobs here, but you're more likely to come across a horse or two.

SAVANNA
Savanna takes its inspiration from the location of the same name in Africa, with its hot temperatures and dry grasslands. The grass is more yellow than in the Plains and the acacia trees give it a different look and feel.

FOREST
Another popular and very common biome is Forest. If you're building a more rural or a fantasy-themed build, Forest takes the open landscape design of the Plains and adds in lots of oak and birch trees.

JUNGLE
If Savanna is a different take on the Plains, then Jungle is a bigger and darker version of Forest. This biome has lots of different types of trees, which vary in height. Jungle is also one of the few biomes where you'll find Temples.

DESERT
The Desert is one of the most unusual biomes. It's very flat, like Plains or Ice Plains, but instead of grassy blocks, you'll find sand and the occasional cactus. Temples are also sometimes found here, as well as strange wells.

REPEAT PROCESS

8 You won't need a Redstone Repeater behind the other Sticky Piston, but you will need to build a similar pattern of Redstone connecting one side to the other. Create a box of sorts, then have them meet by the end at the right-hand side of the trench. Now place a Switch in between both (level with the ground). The line will glow if connected.

BUILD YOUR DOOR

5 The key to the secret lair/base is having a door that reveals the entrance to your new home one moment, and completely conceals it the next. To create this vital feature, you'll need to add some important items to your inventory bar, including the very useful block known as a Sticky Piston.

CONCEAL THE ENTRANCE

9 Now you need to hide all your hard work. Make sure that you don't place blocks on top of the Redstone you've placed, because this will break the circuit. Build around them (leave a hollow gap with the Redstone), including a small step in front of the entrance. Use blocks that match the hill.

START CREATING YOUR ROOMS

3 This all depends on how big you want your base. If you want it to be a small hiding spot when escaping mobs at night, just stick to one small room. But you can build a bunker as large as you'd like. Just remember not to build up too high, because the hill will crumble around you if you do (so be careful).

THE DOOR MECHANISM

6 Place a Sticky Piston to the left of the entrance, one block away and level with the ground. Place a second one on the other side of the door. Again, one block away, but this time it should be one block off the ground. So when both are activated, they will each push a block that will close and reveal the door.

FURNISH YOUR LAIR

4 Just like a house or castle, you're not going to want to go to all the trouble of building a new abode and not fill it with cool stuff. So be sure to equip your new place with some torches, a bed, and some other decorative items in order to ensure your new secret home looks and feels just right (even though you're about to hide it).

USE YOUR REDSTONE

7 Place a Redstone Repeater behind the left Sticky Piston (see pic for correct positioning). Use Redstone to place a red connecting box. Build a trench that's around three blocks long, one wide, and two deep. Place the Redstone and make sure there are no broken links.

DECORATE THE HILL

10 To give the hill an extra layer of believability, you'll need to place some decorations to really hide your new base/lair. Bushes and grass are a great choice, as is a nice tree or two. Just be sure you don't block access to the base itself. You could even add a small marker to help you find it next time.

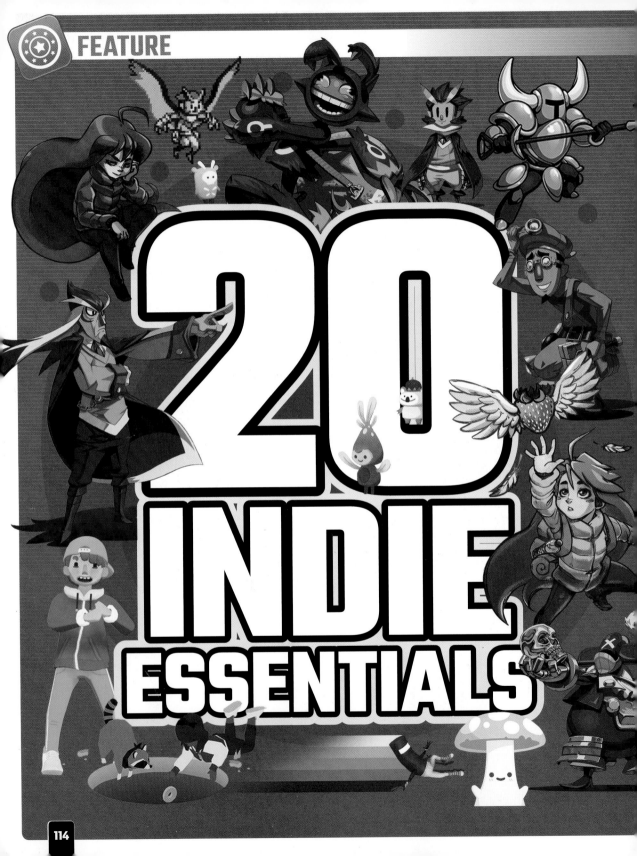

20 INDIE ESSENTIALS

It's been another fantastic year for indie games, delivering a whole host of amazing titles for us to enjoy. In this list of indie highlights, you'll find tricky platformers, beautiful puzzle games, hilarious point-and-clicks, VR stunners, incredible RPGs, and more. In other words, there's something for everyone in this crop of modern classics.

RUNNER3

20

In this fun rhythm-action platformer, you've got to jump, slide, and kick your way through levels in time with the beat of the music. There are extra characters to unlock, secrets to find, and alternative routes to keep levels interesting.

FE

19

Fe is a beautiful 3-D puzzle platformer where you explore a magical forest. Befriend the creatures that live there on your journey and use the special abilities you gain from connecting with them to reach new areas.

GUACAMELEE! 2

18

The sequel to the excellent *Guacamelee!* sees you don the mask of legendary luchador Juan to save the Mexiverse once again. As you play through the game you unlock cool new skills that help you through tough battles and tricky platforming sections.

CHUCHEL

17

Chuchel is a simple game where the focus is on making you laugh. It does have some basic puzzles, but you'll get most of your enjoyment from the strange and funny surprises that the cute little Chuchel meets on every screen.

OWLBOY

16 As you can probably guess from the title of the game, in *Owlboy* you play as a character who can fly. You use this ability to pick up weapons, objects, and even friends to help you solve puzzles and beat bosses.

FAST FACT

Subnautica was originally released via Early Access in 2014. It took until 2018 for it to be ready for full release.

DELTARUNE

15 A spin-off of hit indie title *Undertale*, *Deltarune* is an RPG where you play as two friends named Kris and Susie. You meet many enemies on your adventure, but it's up to you whether you fight or find a peaceful resolution.

* Hey, Kris.
* There's someone up there waving at us.

OOBLETS

14 In this bright and colorful world you can collect and raise cute little creatures called Ooblets, customize your character's look, grow your own farm, decorate your house, and meet other characters in a bustling local town.

THE SWORDS OF DITTO

13 *The Swords of Ditto* is a great introduction into the world of roguelike games. Your goal is to defeat an evil villain within five days. You'll probably fail to finish on your first go, but with each playthrough you'll learn more about the skills and equipment you can find in the game's randomly generated world and what kind of challenges you'll face on your adventure.

SUBNAUTICA

12 You must survive in, and eventually escape, an underwater alien world in this fantastic survival game. You can craft tools and build huge underwater bases and cool submarines as you search for a way to escape the planet.

MOONLIGHTER

11 Every RPG has an item shop filled with potions and elixirs. The twist in *Moonlighter* is that you're the one running it. In addition to managing your shop, you head out on dangerous adventures to find more valuable loot to put up for sale.

MINIT

10 In *Minit* your character must find a way to lift a curse that ends each day after one minute. An adventure game that can only be played in 60-second bursts sounds like it shouldn't work, but this clever title is packed full of fun.

ULTIMATE INDIE CHARACTERS

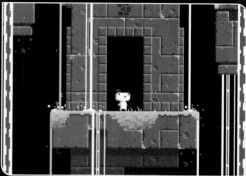

GOMEZ FEZ

He's instantly recognizable thanks to his cool red hat, he's cute, and he's the star of one of the greatest indie platformers ever made.

SHOVEL KNIGHT
SHOVEL KNIGHT

Shovel Knight has become so popular that he's made guest appearances in games such as *Super Smash Bros. Ultimate*.

FRISK
UNDERTALE

Beloved indie RPG *Undertale* has a huge fanbase, so it's no surprise that the game's star, Frisk, is much loved, too.

MADELINE
CELESTE

Madeline is a cute, likeable character, and her struggles with her dark side in *Celeste* tell a powerful story.

CHUCHEL
CHUCHEL

We never get tired of the hilarious sight of the short-tempered Chuchel going mad over losing his precious cherry.

GRIS

9 Explore a beautiful watercolor world in this great platformer. Gris, the young girl you play as, is weak when you start the game. However, as you play and Gris grows along with you, she will gain new abilities that allow her to move around with grace and skill.

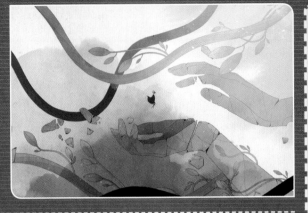

FAR: LONE SAILS

8 In *FAR: Lone Sails* you must run around inside your vehicle, pushing buttons and filling the fuel tanks to keep it going. When the wind picks up, you can raise the sails, take a break, and enjoy the epic scenery you travel past on your journey.

DONUT COUNTY

7 In this fun and silly puzzle game, you play as a hole. Your goal is to try to swallow everything on the screen—cars, chickens, telescopes, or even whole buildings—as you grow ever bigger.

LASER LEAGUE

6 If you're looking for games to play with friends, *Laser League* is one of the best. The goal is to capture nodes that create walls of light in your team's color to take out the other team, while dodging their color.

MOSS

5 One of the best VR titles out there, *Moss* is a game where you help a little mouse named Quill save his kingdom. You can move things around in the environment to help Quill make his way through the world.

INTO THE BREACH

4 *Into The Breach* is a tricky turn-based strategy game, but very rewarding once you get to grips with it. You can always see what your opponent is going to do next, so the idea is to think ahead and plan the perfect counter.

YOKU'S ISLAND EXPRESS

3 A unique blend of pinball and platforming, *Yoku's Island Express* is a game where you fire a dung beetle named Yoku around the island of Mokumana using pinball paddles. It's a cool idea that mixes well with traditional platforming and fun exploration.

FAST FACT

There are 80 hidden Wickerlings for you to collect in *Yoku's Island Express.* Can you find every single one?

EXPERT COMMENT
MATTIA TRAVERSO
Lead designer behind *Last Day of June*

How do you tell a story with a game?
Most of the indie devs from 2018 (and now, 2019) seemed to be concerned with this question. Few though hit the nail on the head as *Florence* did. The game's apparent simplicity might ward you off at first, but that'd be a mistake. Its simplicity hides true elegance and depth: *Florence* is interactive poetry perfected. It's a game that relishes in being a video game and expresses so much of the love and growth of the two characters with the game design. A poignant, sweet little interactive gem.

THE GARDENS BETWEEN

2 *The Gardens Between* stars two friends called Arina and Frendt. Instead of controlling the pair to guide them through the island gardens they are exploring, you control time and use it to change the environment to help the duo through.

CELESTE

1 *Celeste* is one of the best platformers we've played in years. Telling the story of Madeline's quest to climb a huge mountain, the game tests you with some rock-hard platforming challenges on your way to the mountain's summit. You'll fail a lot, but sticking with the game and overcoming seemingly impossible tasks time and time again feels amazing. If you do find the game too tricky, it's got a fantastic difficulty system that lets you choose from several assists to make the experience a bit friendlier.

FAST FACT

This is the first EA Sports game to include the official UEFA Champions League license since *UEFA Champions League 2006–2007.*

FIFA 19
WE ARE THE CHAMPIONS

The big new feature in *FIFA 19* is the return of the UEFA Champions League, enabling you to compete against the best teams in Europe. The tournament features a brand-new presentation suite and set of commentators, and this also extends to Career Mode, giving you the chance to dominate the competition with your favorite club. Elsewhere, story mode "The Journey" reaches its final chapter in the saga of Alex Hunter, Kim Hunter, and Danny Williams, while Ultimate Team introduces key new features. Even Kick-Off mode has received an overhaul, providing more ways to compete against your friends. You can force players to score in specific ways or turn off the rules!

QUICK TIPS!

LEARN FROM THE BEST
The Champions Channel in Ultimate Team enables you to watch full replays of top-level games to help improve your skills.

USE DYNAMIC TACTICS
You can use Dynamic Tactics to customize team instructions and roles, as well as set up offensive and defensive game plans.

MASTER TIMED FINISHING
To hit a super-accurate shot, power it up and then press shoot again just before you kick the ball.

TOP 5

UEFA CHAMPIONS LEAGUE TEAMS

1 JUVENTUS

This Italian Serie A side boasts *FIFA 19*'s cover star among its ranks: Cristiano Ronaldo. The Portuguese player is one of many talented players at Juventus, with others including Paulo Dybala, Giorgio Chiellini, and French World Cup winner Blaise Matuidi.

2 BARCELONA

Lionel Messi is the joint-highest-rated player in the game, with Ronaldo, and plays for Barcelona. The Argentinian boasts outstanding skills, so try getting the ball to him as often as you can.

3 MANCHESTER CITY

With Sergio Agüero, David Silva, and Kevin De Bruyne, it shouldn't be hard to win the Champions League with Man City, who have won multiple Premier League titles recently.

4 REAL MADRID

This La Liga team have won the most UEFA Champions League trophies (formerly the European Cup) in history, including five in a row, from 1956–1960. Star players are Luka Modrić and Gareth Bale.

5 BAYERN MUNICH

The best Bundesliga side in *FIFA 19* is Bayern Munich, taking advantage of Manuel Neuer in goal and Robert Lewandowski in attack. FC Bayern are the most successful German team in history.

ALSO CHECK OUT ...

PRO EVOLUTION SOCCER 2019
This great soccer series from Konami is *FIFA*'s biggest rival.

FOOTBALL MANAGER 2019
Think you could be a manager? Prove it!

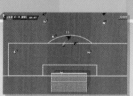

SUPER ARCADE FOOTBALL
A fast-paced soccer game with a host of fun modes.

FAST FACT

Madden esports keeps getting bigger and bigger, with the Madden NFL 19 Championship Series awarding an $1.255 million in prizing!

MADDEN NFL 19

ANOTHER WINNING PLAY

Madden might be the only football sim in town, but EA Sports didn't coast on its long-running success with this latest version. Exhibiting clear improvement over last year's game, *Madden NFL 19* quickly showcases its upgrades. Animation is improved and more fluid gameplay is provided by the Real Player Motion system, which leads a raft of new tweaks and additions. Even so, the end result is still undeniably *Madden*, delivering an accessible-yet-realistic take on the sport with loads of fun modes (like Madden Ultimate Team). It has an uncanny ability to make you feel just like a pro quarterback, wide receiver, or whatever other position you most prefer. There's a reason that this series has endured for more than 30 years!

QUICK TIPS!

QUICK AUDIBLES
Hit L2 or the left trigger in Playbook Formations to choose which audibles are quickly available when you want to switch up a play.

SWAP STYLES
You can choose between Arcade, Simulation, and Competitive play styles, each of which provides a significantly different experience.

USE QB SLIDE
If you're running as the QB and about to be pulverized by the competition, be sure to slide—you'll protect both your player and the ball.

TOP ★★★ 5 NEW FEATURES

1 REAL PLAYER MOTION

Thanks to a completely redesigned locomotion system, the players in *Madden NFL 19* look better than ever in motion. They run and jostle realistically as they crash into rivals and make winning catches.

2 MORE CONTROL, TOO

Real Player Motion is about more than just looks. It also impacts the way the game feels and plays. "Push the Pile" lets you eke out extra yards with the right stick due to the enhanced animation.

3 LET'S CELEBRATE

Madden NFL 19 lets you choose from a few different celebration moves after a touchdown, sack, or any other big play. One option even lets you steal a signature move from the other team. Spicy!

4 LONGER SHOT

Back for more after the previous game, the Longshot: Homecoming story mode lets you control the destiny of two different players. Plus it's packed with four times the gameplay moments for a more immersive experience.

5 SOLO BATTLES

Are you looking for steady competition in Madden Ultimate Team without always playing online? *Madden NFL 19*'s Solo Battles provide 13 games per week to play with your created card-based team.

ALSO CHECK OUT ...

FIFA 19
EA's smash soccer sim has its own engrossing Ultimate Team mode.

PYRE
This fantasy role-player revolves around a unique and fun team sport.

SUPER MEGA BASEBALL 2
Create your own team and players, then try to dominate the league.

FAST FACT

NBA 2K, the series' first entry, was a Sega Dreamcast exclusive, but the later version *NBA 2K2* was the first version to expand to other consoles.

NBA 2K19
GREATEST OF ALL TIME

NBA 2K19 marks the series' 20th anniversary. For two decades now, this hoops series has towered over the competition. That's never been more true than with *NBA 2K19*, which delivers an even more polished and precise basketball simulation, with stunningly lifelike renditions of LeBron James, Kevin Durant, and other top stars. There's no better-looking sports game in the world, but *NBA 2K19*

also delivers in the gameplay as a realistic sim that's easy to pick up and play. Even if you're not a die-hard basketball fan, you can drop threes and dominate in no time. With in-depth franchise and story options, the street play of Neighborhood mode, and loads of classic teams, it's the ultimate b-ball experience!

QUICK TIPS!

PLAY DAILY FOR VC
Make sure you perform the free daily wheel spin and complete as many daily objectives as you can to earn some bonus VC currency.

SNAG BADGES
Embrace the grind! The more you play and work on your core skills, the more you'll earn attribute badges that boost your created player's stats.

PICK A BAD TEAM
No, really! In MyCareer, your created player probably won't get much court time on a top NBA team—so choose a losing squad instead.

TOP 5 ★★★

BIGGEST IMPROVEMENTS

2 EXTRA POLISH

Yes, *NBA 2K* games always look fantastic, but this year's entry adds a lot of extra detail missing from the previous game, especially when it comes to player models not clipping into each other.

1 TAKEOVER TIME

You know how the NBA's elite players can totally take over a game at times? That's what the Takeover system emulates. Play well to fill up a meter and you'll get a stat boost to help you own the court.

3 A TRIP TO CHINA

The MyCareer mode comes with a neat twist this time around: You'll start off in China as an undrafted rookie, where you'll feel like a fish out of water as you try to thrive and succeed in the unfamiliar setting.

4 A THRIVING 'HOOD

The Neighborhood mode feels much more alive, with more hype in the street ball mode, including live events, extra activities, a much-improved layout, and enhanced player progression.

5 SERIOUSLY SMART AI

The computer players see a serious intelligence boost with realistic strategies and reactions to your own moves. That might make them trickier to outwit, but it also makes the game a lot more satisfying.

ALSO CHECK OUT...

NBA 2K PLAYGROUNDS 2
This arcade-style spin-off game is like a modern version of *NBA Jam*.

WINDJAMMERS
Test your reflexes with this fast-paced, cult-classic arcade game.

BOUNCY HOOPS
Never stop hoopin' with this super enjoyable endless mobile game.

MARIO TENNIS ACES

FAST FACT

Mario Tennis Aces is the first Mario sports game to include a story mode since Mario Tennis: Power Tour in 2005.

SMASHING ARCADE TENNIS GAME

When it comes to sports with Mario and the gang, you know you're in for fun. From golf to baseball to tennis, when the crew from the Mushroom Kingdom get involved, it's gonna be a blast. That's why the Nintendo Switch's Mario Tennis Aces is one of the greatest sports games on the console! Complete various stages of challenging tennis as you work to capture the legendary tennis racket Lucien, who's possessed both Wario and Waluigi. When you're done checking out Adventure Mode you can challenge friends online and test your tennis skills out against other Mario Tennis Aces players to see who comes out on top. It's an action-packed twist on the world of tennis you've gotta play.

QUICK TIPS!

DON'T WASTE THOSE ZONE SHOTS!

It's tempting to use a Zone Shot immediately, but save them for when you're really in a pinch!

STUDY EACH CHARACTER

Each character has a set of powerful abilities and weaknesses, so study them all to exploit them!

USE TRICK SHOTS

Trick shots don't use up energy, so sub them in when you think you need a Power Shot instead!

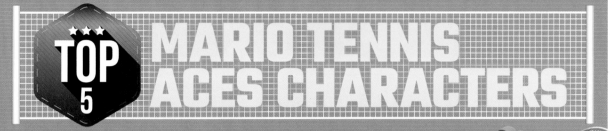

TOP 5 MARIO TENNIS ACES CHARACTERS

1 BOO
Boo's a real nightmare for your opponents—and not just because he's a ghost! The spooky spirit can add some serious curve to his serves, making it difficult to return them.

2 BOWSER JR.
If you want to return your opponent's serves, you've got to get to the ball, quick! Bowser Jr. can cover plenty of ground fast with his floating contraption, so other players have to work harder.

3 YOSHI
When it comes to speeding around the court, no one's faster than Yoshi, that adorable green dinosaur. He'll zoom over to the ball and have it back over the net faster than you can say "trick shot."

CHAIN CHOMP 4
Speedy returns and versatile movement during matches is useful, but sometimes you need to smash a shot that the other player simply can't hit back. Chain Chomp is capable of delivering those shots every time, no sweat!

5 MARIO
Our main man Mario is an all-round great guy and, as it turns out, he's an all-round great player on the tennis court, too! He's a pretty balanced player with stats that should help all players succeed, whatever their level!

ALSO CHECK OUT . . .

MARIO TENNIS OPEN
Challenge Mario and friends on the go in this fun tennis game on the 3DS.

SEGA SUPERSTARS TENNIS
Sega's coolest characters duke it out on the court.

MARIO KART 8 DELUXE
Mario characters go head-to-head in kooky kart races!

TOP 10

AR GAMES
BLUR THE BOUNDARIES BETWEEN REAL AND VIRTUAL LIFE

1 MY TAMAGOTCHI FOREVER

Japanese toy maker Bandai released Tamagotchi in 1996, but look at how it's grown. This modern twist adds augmented reality within a hide-and-seek mini-game, so as well as trying to keep your virtual creature alive, you can explore TamaTown to find friends, hidden treasures, and cool bonuses.

2 KINGS OF POOL

You probably don't have space for a full-sized pool table in your home, but this game for iOS and Android makes it possible. It uses augmented reality to place a virtual table in your room, enabling you to walk around and position yourself before tapping, dragging back the cue, and potting those balls just as you would in real life.

FAST FACT

Pokémon GO is integrated within the Nintendo Switch games Pokémon: Let's Go, Pikachu!, and Pokémon: Let's Go, Eevee!

3 TETROIDS AR PUZZLE GAME

Tetroids AR makes use of iOS's built-in ARKit to put a fresh spin on the classic Russian puzzler Tetris. It lays falling blocks on to any real surface in your immediate environment, letting you slot them into place to clear rows and make combos to rack up the points. A rendition of the well-known Tetris tune, Korobeiniki, also plays.

4 AR ROBOT

Do your parents send you to your room because you won't stop squabbling? Bad move! Launch AR Robot on an iOS device and you can let battle commence on your bedroom floor instead. Train, customize, and level-up your virtual robot (there are 100 million combos), then let it compete in a one-on-one fight. You can even battle against a buddy's bot online.

5 THE BIRDCAGE

Stick this beautiful yet logical puzzle game into AR mode, and a series of 26 golden birdcages will spring up from the ground. Your task is to find keys by solving puzzles and riddles, enabling you to release the ocean-colored birds contained within each one—a task that is much harder than it sounds.

6 POKÉMON GO

Nintendo refreshed the *Pokémon* franchise when it launched this huge multiplayer, location-based offering in 2016. It remains as fun an experience as it did when millions of people raced around the streets looking for little critters. Many new additions have helped, including PvP mode.

7 KID ICARUS: UPRISING

This third-person shooter let Nintendo 3DS owners scan AR cards using the handheld's outer camera to produce Idols that could battle one another. In December 2018, Nintendo released a previously unseen AR card on its Twitter accounts. Check it out at https://bit.ly/2YM5Dpd.

8 LEGO BRICKHEADZ BUILDER AR

This app lets you create LEGO BrickHeadz characters and build virtual versions of LEGO products in the real world via an Android device. With no in-app purchases, simply play with your creations, compete in mini-games, unlock new characters, and unleash your imagination in a free-build section.

9 CLASH & GO: AR STRATEGY

Powered by blockchain technology and combining open-world geolocation with augmented reality, *Clash & GO* overlays objects onto the real world and enables you to build cities and take part in gripping real-time battles to capture local landmarks.

EXPERT COMMENT
ALAN YEATS
Developer and cofounder of Pocket Sized Hands

Augmented reality brings a new, immersive aspect to the way we consume games. AR games bring the characters and objects to life, giving the illusion of the game world being in the room with you. This brings in so many more possibilities on what we as game developers can build for our players and the worlds these games can take place within.

10 RUN AN EMPIRE

If anybody has ever told you to stop playing games and get some exercise, then tell them you can do both. Simply install *Run an Empire* and you can run, jog, or walk to capture local lands and add them to your empire. What's more is that as you make your way around your locality, you can also earn coins.

THREE TOP AR PLATFORMS
There are a few devices that allow you to enjoy augmented reality games.

IOS
Apple has certainly put a lot of time, money, and effort into augmented reality, and it claims to have the biggest AR platform in the world. ARKit 2 for iOS 12 makes it possible for multiple users to play a game, which enhances the experience and can be even more fun.

ANDROID
Google's software development kit, ARCore, is available for a number of Android smartphones, and it makes it much easier for developers to produce AR games. It means that smartphones can make sense of the real world via the camera.

MICROSOFT HOLOLENS
Still under development, Microsoft HoloLens is a pair of mixed-reality smartglasses that allow users to see and interact with virtual 3-D images. These are overlaid onto a real-life environment surrounding the wearer.

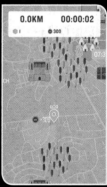

FAST FACT

The original *Spelunky* was created by one man, Derek Yu, and originally available for free on Windows before it became a huge hit.

SPELUNKY 2

ADVENTURING FOR TREASURE

Following in the footsteps of the classic *Spelunky*, *Spelunky 2* returns us to a world of exciting underground platforming. As with the first game, levels are randomly generated, so the game is different every time you play. Each time you fail, you must start again, so your goal is to get better at the game and learn more about how it works until you finally manage a successful run all the way to the end.

Spelunky 2 is packed full of secrets for you to discover, but as any experienced spelunker knows, there are also loads of deadly traps, so make sure you keep your eyes open at all times. And try to avoid making any silly mistakes that will send you all the way back to the beginning.

QUICK TIPS!

TRY EVERYTHING
Test every new item or object you come across to see what it does. Knowledge is power in *Spelunky*.

DON'T GET COMFORTABLE
Once you start to get good at the game, it's easy to stop paying proper attention and get taken out by basic traps and enemies.

FAILURE IS FINE
You are supposed to fail in *Spelunky*. It's how you learn. So don't let it get you down.

NEW VERSUS OLD

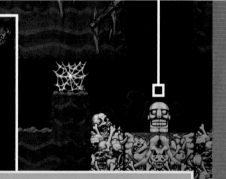

SHOPPING FOR SUCCESS

Buying items from stores to help you on your adventure can be a very important part of a successful run. It might take a few playthroughs before you know what each item does, though.

IT'S A TRAP

That golden head might look tempting, but watch out for the trap set up above it. *Spelunky* loves to tempt you with treasure like this, so it's important to always keep your guard up and pay attention to what's around you.

NEW DIMENSION

What you see here is only one layer of the level. New to *Spelunky 2* is the ability to move between two layers on each level, opening up some cool new possibilities for exploration.

NEW ROSTER

The new *Spelunky* has new characters for us to play as: Ana Spelunky, Roffy D. Sloth, Margaret Tunnel, and Colin Northwood. You can team up with friends to play locally or online.

ALSO CHECK OUT ...

CRYPT OF THE NECRODANCER
Mixing randomly generated levels with rhythm action.

ENTER THE GUNGEON
Action-packed fun where the game is different every time you play.

CELESTE
For fans of tough platforming games, this one definitely fits the bill.

PICTURE THIS!

GET TO KNOW . . . ROBLOX!

FAST FACT

There are lots of *Roblox* events around the world for fans and developers, including conventions and competitions.

ROBLOX COMMUNITY

Almost every kind of game in *Roblox* involves sharing a world with other players in the game. The number of players can change, but you'll most likely find someone else to play with at any time. You can become friends with them, too!

YOUR ROBLOX AVATAR

This is your avatar. He—or she—might not look like much now, but spend a little time in the game and you'll soon get to know *Roblox*'s customization options. You can purchase new outfits, download ones from toys you've bought, or unlock them in games.

MENU OPTIONS

These buttons on the bottom of the screen differ depending on the game you're playing, and each one will give you lots of options to play with. For instance, here you can choose to add furniture to your restaurant, choose when to open it, and more.

1   2   3   4

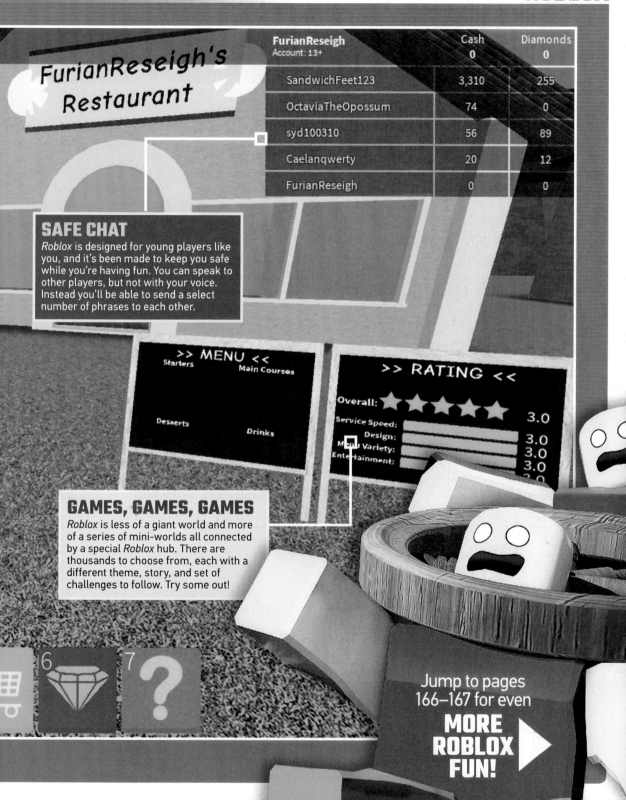

FurianReseigh's Restaurant

FurianReseigh	Cash	Diamonds
Account: 13+	0	0
SandwichFeet123	3,310	255
OctaviaTheOpossum	74	0
syd100310	56	89
Caelanqwerty	20	12
FurianReseigh	0	0

SAFE CHAT

Roblox is designed for young players like you, and it's been made to keep you safe while you're having fun. You can speak to other players, but not with your voice. Instead you'll be able to send a select number of phrases to each other.

>> MENU <<
Starters   Main Courses
Desserts   Drinks

>> RATING <<
Overall: ★★★★★
Service Speed: 3.0
Design: 3.0
Menu Variety: 3.0
Entertainment: 3.0
                              3.0

GAMES, GAMES, GAMES

Roblox is less of a giant world and more of a series of mini-worlds all connected by a special *Roblox* hub. There are thousands to choose from, each with a different theme, story, and set of challenges to follow. Try some out!

Jump to pages 166–167 for even

MORE ROBLOX FUN! ▶

FAST FACT

The Wisp power-ups first made their series debut in *Sonic Colors*. Aliens from the Planet Wisp, they're composed of an energy force!

TEAM SONIC RACING

GOTTA GO FAST!

Sonic and the gang are all revved up and ready to go in *Team Sonic Racing*. Characters from the *Sonic* universe—such as the Blue Blur himself, plus Tails, Knuckles, Shadow, Amy Rose, and more—have joined up for a team-based kart racing game where the winner takes all. With awesome new Wisp-based power-ups, lots of fun *Sonic* moments, and speedy new karts, fans will have plenty to dig into with this new *Sonic* racer. From the starting line to the finish, tackle radical new tracks, groove along to familiar *Sonic* music, and earn extra points based on your finishing position.

QUICK TIPS!

WORK WITH YOUR BUDDIES
Work closely with your team to support each racer and you'll be on your way to victory in no time.

TRY OUT EVERY RACER
Get to know every racer in *Team Sonic Racing* so you're experienced with all of them in every situation.

DON'T SLEEP ON THE WISPS
Each Wisp has a unique power-up. Make sure you're making proper use of them!

NEED FOR SPEED

AWESOME ARENAS

There are plenty of different race tracks to enjoy in *Team Sonic Racing*, from Boo's House to Market Street, and plenty of other awesome locations. You'll have seen some of them before in previous *Sonic* games, too!

ALL YOUR FRIENDS ARE HERE

It's a huge *Sonic* reunion, with more racers in the game than ever before. From Team Sonic's Sonic, Tails, and Knuckles to Team Rose with Amy, Big the Cat, and Chao, all your faves are here—yep, even Metal Sonic!

RADICAL POWERS

Team Sonic Racing has a ton of different power-ups and items you can use with your crew to make sure you take first place. Colorful Wisps will grant powers that can help you speed up or enhance the way you race.

SUPERSONIC TUNES

Team Sonic Racing has a ton of sizzling new *Sonic* tracks, with music by the songwriter and popular *Sonic* collaborator Jun Senoue, of Crush 40. There are also fun remixes of classic tunes! Ready for a *Sonic* dance party?

ALSO CHECK OUT ...

SONIC & ALL-STARS RACING TRANSFORMED
Sonic and assorted Sega characters hit the track!

CRASH TEAM RACING NITRO-FUELED
Gaming's most notorious Bandicoot behind the wheel.

MARIO KART 8 DELUXE
Mario and friends race each other in crazy kart battles!

FAST FACT

Including your own created characters and different character versions, there are an incredible 162 characters you can play as in LEGO *DC Super-Villains*.

LEGO DC SUPER-VILLAINS

BAD TO THE BONE

Sometimes it's fun to be the bad guy—LEGO *DC Super-Villains* is perfect proof of that. You form the ultimate team of super-villains in a quest to defeat another team of super-villains, posing as heroes, from an alternate dimension. The game has a huge roster of great baddies from the DC Universe for you to unlock and play as, including The Joker, Harley Quinn, Lex Luthor, and many more. You also get to create your own super-villain, customize their look, and choose their special powers to aid you on an adventure full of action, puzzles, and the laugh-out-loud humor the LEGO games are known for.

QUICK TIPS!

USE JOHNNY DC

If you're not sure where to go next and feel like you need some guidance, click on the left stick and Johnny DC will give you a helping hand.

COLLECT EVERY STUD

Collect every stud you can find—you can use them to unlock cool stuff in-game.

MIX AND MATCH

Try switching between different villains to test out their moves and see which ones are best suited to different situations and play styles.

THE BUILDING BLOCKS OF SUCCESS

GET 'EM ALL

For fans of the comics, there's nothing more satisfying that seeing just how many characters from the DC Universe there are for you to play as. As well as this pair— Cheetah and Solomon Grundy—there's a massive roster to unlock.

JOKER'S PARADISE

Fitting with the fun LEGO look, expect lots of jokes, parodies, and references to keep things lighthearted and keep you laughing along as you play through the game.

SIGHTSEEING

The game features a mix of open world–style gameplay (meaning you can go where you please) and more structured story missions. You can visit iconic DC locations including Gotham City and Metropolis.

PICK AND CHOOSE

You can swap between characters whenever you like. Sometimes this is just for fun, but sometimes you'll also need to use a specific power to solve a puzzle or remove an obstacle.

ALSO CHECK OUT ...

LEGO MARVEL SUPER HEROES 2
Another comic book LEGO game, this time with Marvel characters.

SKYLANDERS: IMAGINATORS
A cool mix of game styles, just like the LEGO series.

SUPER SMASH BROS. ULTIMATE
If you like a big roster of characters, this is for you.

DRAGON BALL FIGHTERZ

YOU NEED PRACTICE. JUST SAIYAN!

Dragon Ball fans rejoice! If you want a game featuring all your favorite characters, with graphics that could have been pulled straight from the TV show, this is exactly what you've been looking for. It's a fighting game that feels as good as it looks.

Dragon Ball FighterZ is a 3v3 tag-team fighter with an all-new story to experience. If you want to jump straight in to the fights, no problem! You can ignore the story and fight against the CPU or a friend offline, or take your skills online and show the world what you're made of.

Choose your favorite characters and find an opponent—you don't want to be all dressed up with nowhere to Goku.

QUICK TIPS!

DASH IT ALL
You can dash both on the ground and in the air. Remember, you can dash backward to avoid certain attacks.

WHERE'D YOU GO?
If you have at least one bar on your Ki meter, you can Vanish Attack to teleport behind your opponent.

TEAMS WORK
Trigger a Super, then (with enough Ki) hit an assist button for a teammate to jump in with their Super!

YOU'RE KRILLIN IT

DON'T FEEL BLUE

When you've started to take damage, you'll notice that some of your health bar turns blue. This is health that you can recover. One way to do this is to tag your current character out—they'll slowly heal in reserve.

FAST FRIENDS

Bringing a team of three into battle means you can switch between characters any time (so long as they have health left), or you can call a buddy like Krillin here to jump in with an attack to help out!

Vegeta (Super Saiyan)

233

Cell

Assist!
Counter!

3

MY WORD

On-screen notifications will give you information to help you understand what you're doing right . . . or wrong. Here, Vegeta calling in Krillin not only triggers an Assist attack, but this attack has also countered one of his opponent's. Tough luck, Cell!

KI GOING

This is your Ki gauge. The maximum level is seven—different actions need different levels. An EX version of one of your specials needs one bar, for example, while a Super can use anything from one to seven.

ALSO CHECK OUT . . .

DRAGON BALL XENOVERSE 2
A *Dragon Ball* game with aerial fights and role-playing.

NARUTO SHIPPUDEN: ULTIMATE NINJA STORM 4: ROAD TO BORUTO
A gorgeous-looking anime fighter that will blow you away.

DRAGON BALL FUSIONS
Make your very own characters in this handheld *Dragon Ball* adventure.

ULTIMATE GAMER CHALLENGE!

Think you've got the gaming skills to throw down with the masters? Then prove it! Our experts have picked out a selection of cool challenges for anyone who fancies themselves as a gaming legend. How many of these tricky trials will you be able to conquer? Each is designed to help develop skills that can extend beyond a single game and make you a better player in general, so fire up a game and show us what you can do!

POWER UP!

TASKS MASTERED

You don't need to get the best rank on the various Taskmaster Challenges to unlock everything, but why not try anyway? Each requires different sets of skills—from working out fast routes to mastering combat systems, this will really help you improve your general gaming skills!

MARVEL'S SPIDER-MAN SENSATIONAL!

This awesome action game is no joke—even on the Spectacular setting—so it'll take a brave hero to try to beat it on Ultimate difficulty! Save this challenge for a second playthrough, once you know the enemy attack patterns and have a proper grasp of how all of Spidey's moves slot together.

MONSTER HUNTER: WORLD
TEMPER, TEMPER

The brutal beasts of *Monster Hunter* are usually designed to be beaten by groups of players. If your skills and gear are up to it, though, tell your Palico to stay at home and go after a Tempered Elder Dragon solo. Vaal Hazak is the easiest of the bunch—as long as your armor can withstand its rotten breath. Gross!

TIME ATTACK
CRASH BANDICOOT
N.SANE TRILOGY

The High Road is one of the toughest levels in the original *Crash Bandicoot*. Can you beat our best Time Trial run of 1:02:29 and grab a Platinum Relic of your own?

YU-GI-OH! DUEL LINKS
MESSING WITH THE META

Some people spend a lot of time and money putting together what they think are unbeatable decks in this mobile card game. Prove them wrong by assembling your own deck rather than building one based on an existing list, then gunning for the King of Games rank. Good luck!

FINAL FANTASY XIV: SHADOWBRINGERS
MASTER BUILDERS UNITE!

Want to make the best items in *Final Fantasy XIV*? Here's how . . .

1 First of all, you'll need to raise a crafting job to the maximum level. Doing this just by making things normally will take you absolutely ages, so use Levequests and collectable turn-ins to speed the process along.

2 Next: Time to gear up. The best crafting gear is always expensive on the Market Board, but the Handking set can be earned by turning in Yellow Scrips, so aim for that.

3 More leveling now, as you'll need a few extra skills from the other crafters. You don't need to take most of these past level 50, but abilities like Innovation and Muscle Memory are vital.

4 You're all set. Even the toughest recipes will be no match for you now, so get busy; making some cool stuff might just help you unlock your own abilities.

SCORE ATTACK

TETRIS EFFECT
Get in the zone! Can you clear the whole screen at once during Zone mode to earn a Perfectris? Only true puzzle masters will manage this!

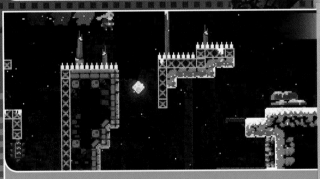

CELESTE BERRY DIFFICULT
Collecting strawberries doesn't actually unlock anything in the game, but it might just help you unlock your own abilities. Each will teach you how to stretch your platforming abilities to their limits, and respawns are pretty generous, so there's no reason not to try and grab the lot.

POWER UP!

TAPE ESCAPE
Finding the hidden cassettes in each stage grants access to the hidden B-Side versions of levels, and they're all super difficult. Can you unlock and clear them all?

POWER UP!

YOU ARE THE CREW

To take that pirate challenge to the next level, why not see if you can pull it off solo in your own little sloop? Hoist the sails at the first time of danger—you'll never outgun a galleon in that little thing!

SEA OF THIEVES HOLD FULL OF GOLD!

Arrr, matey! Can ye fill yer hold with as much booty as it can carry and safely make port with all yer loot without some scurvy dogs making off with the lot? Keep a lookout fer trouble as ye sail home!

EXPERT CHALLENGE!

THE LEGEND OF ZELDA: BREATH OF THE WILD

Are you the true hero of Hyrule? Prove yourself worthy of the title by rushing to the castle and beating Master mode in under an hour.

MINECRAFT SLEEPLESS KNIGHT

Most speedrunners use exploding beds to make quick work of *Minecraft*'s Ender Dragon, but there's no honor in that! Instead, stock up on arrows and take the fight to the big beast properly, and make sure your armor can take a few hits, too.

LABO DO IT YOURSELF

Nintendo's cardboard creation kits are great fun, but the best part is that you can think outside the box and develop your own builds using the Toy-Con Garage mode. Let your imagination run wild and make something truly awesome.

POWER UP!

SPIRITED AWAY

For the ultimate challenge, head into a Spirit Battle without actually equipping a Spirit team of your own. Your damage will be super low, so you'll need to chip away at opponents carefully to secure a win like this!

SUPER SMASH BROS. ULTIMATE
GOTTA CATCH 'EM ALL!

Have you unlocked all of the playable fighters yet? A pop-up message will let you know when you have done that. So if you haven't seen that, keep playing! Some appear when certain conditions are met, but all will also eventually challenge you after a set number of matches.

CHALLENGE TIME

ONRUSH

Score a win for your team in this cool combat racer by wiping out the entire enemy team in a single use of your powerful Rush ability!

LEGO DC SUPER-VILLAINS
THE GOOD GUYS ALWAYS WIN!

Ignore the title and try to beat as many stages as possible in Free Play mode using only hero characters—no villains allowed! You might need to unlock quite a few first, just to ensure that you have access to all the required powers and abilities.

TOP 5 COOLEST CHALLENGES!

STREET FIGHTER V
BACKING THE UNDERDOG

It's too easy to just pick Ryu or Ken. Instead, challenge yourself to get wins with trickier characters like Dhalsim and FANG . . . it's a whole lot more rewarding when you do, and nobody expects to have to fight them!

SUPER MARIO ODYSSEY
SKIP TO THE END

Being able to hop off Cappy after throwing him opens up some super-cool expert movement options that can allow you to skip huge sections of levels and grab some Moons early. Give it a go!

SUPER METROID
HOW LOW CAN YOU GO?

Many speedrun games have categories called low%, where the goal is to beat the game with as few upgrades as possible. Think you can beat this classic Nintendo adventure without picking up any extra health or missile tanks? Good luck . . .

POKÉMON ULTRA SUN/MOON
THE LIVING POKEDEX

It's not enough to just *see* every Pokémon. Real masters keep one of every single species—in numerical order—in the PC box, a truly complete collection of every monster in the game. Bonus points for keeping extras of each variant as well!

KINGDOM HEARTS II
LEVEL DOWN?!

Start on the crazy-tough Critical difficulty and equip the EXP Zero ability as soon as possible—the goal is to finish the game on the hardest setting without ever leveling up. It's some hardcore Disney action!

Crazy — SUPER
Funky — GOOD
Sunny — OK

JUST DANCE 2019
WILD WORKOUT

Games like this are a great way to exercise and stay healthy, so why not put your moves to good use and dance your way to fitness? Try to make it through every song in the game, but be sure to take breaks whenever you find yourself short of breath.

STARLINK: BATTLE FOR ATLAS
TAKING STOCK

Sure, the game is all about adding extra crafts and weapons via cool toys, but you don't *need* them. Prove that by blasting all the way through the game using only the basic ship and weapons—you can go crazy with all those awesome extras afterward.

POWER UP!
NUZLOCKE RUNS

This fan-created self-imposed challenge involved catching only the first new Pokémon you see in each area and depositing any that faint in battle into the PC, making for a wild ride! Are you up to the task?

POKÉMON: LET'S GO, PIKACHU! AND EEVEE! WINNING STREAK

Unlike most *Pokémon* games, wild monsters in *Let's Go* actually appear in the field. Thanks to this, it's possible to clock up huge catching streaks of the same Pokémon—and the longer your streak, the higher the odds of getting good stats, or even a shiny version! Get that counter to 50, trainers!

FORZA HORIZON 4
BARN THIS WAY

Who on earth leaves fancy old supercars to rust away in dirty old barns? Never mind that—finders keepers! Tracking down every Barn Find will include those that are exclusive to specific seasons, so you'll need to play the year around to claim the lot.

EXPERT CHALLENGE!
DRAGON BALL FIGHTERZ

Send your opponent to a world of hurt by landing a 100-hit combo! You'll likely need to use all three characters and a bunch of Supers to pull this off . . .

SPYRO REIGNITED TRILOGY
SPEEDY SPYRO

There are a ton of secrets to find and dragons to rescue, but forget about all that—how fast can you complete the first game? Anything under one hour is a really good time (and doable once you learn the levels), but the fastest players have managed in-game times of under 30 minutes!

SOULCALIBUR VI
BLADES OF GLORY

Unlock the best weapons by mastering styles in Libra of Souls mode.

1 Start by **creating a new fighter.** You can assign a **starting fighting style here** but your character **can wield any weapon** they find, so try to make **sure that** you find and use something that looks cool!

3 Once you have managed that (and after you've progressed far enough throughout the story), Edge Master will give you a new mission to defeat that weapon's master spirit.

2 Using a weapon type will slowly level your affinity with its **original** owner's soul. Keep fighting with your newly acquired weapon and you'll eventually max out this gauge.

4 The battles are challenging, but if you can beat these tough opponents, you'll be rewarded with some amazingly powerful new weapons.

POWER UP!
PICKY EATER

For the purpose of this challenge, you can only grow one type of crop each season. Choose wisely or you might run out of money before the year is out!

STARDEW VALLEY TOP OF THE CROPS

Farming can be surprisingly profitable, especially when you know the right crops to plant and when. Grab new seeds whenever you can and try to earn a small fortune. Keep spending low and you'll amass millions in no time!

TIME ATTACK
MARIO KART 8 DELUXE

Endurance race time! Think you can get through all 48 tracks in under 2.5 hours? Then prove it! Cross your fingers for no Blue Shells.

TOP 5 GAME-BREAKERS & GLITCHES

POKÉMON RED/BLUE
ELITE CHEAT

By perform a string of specific menu manipulation tricks, it's possible to complete the game before even obtaining your first Pokémon with an in-game time of zero minutes. Who even figured this out?!

DONKEY KONG COUNTRY: TROPICAL FREEZE
ROLLING THUNDER

It's not *technically* a glitch, but rolling off ledges allows you to jump in mid-air just as you leave the edge for extra speed and distance. These jumps can be chained together to keep gaining speed. Using this trick allows you to skip tricky sections and finish levels in record time!

SONIC BOOM
FLY, KNUCKLES, FLY!

In the original release of the game, there was a bug where pausing the game refreshed Knuckles' double-jump ability, meaning he could jump forever. Yes, even right over entire levels! This has since been patched, so don't waste your time trying it now . . .

PORTAL
OUT OF BOUNDS

Watch a speedrun of *Portal* and you'll notice that players spend more time outside levels than in them. Sneaky portal placement lets you leave the intended play space, leading to a possible completion time of under ten minutes for the whole game!

THE LEGEND OF ZELDA: BREATH OF THE WILD
WHISTLE WHILE YOU WALK

Here's an easy glitch you can try yourself. Hold the whistle button down, then tap the run button rapidly while moving and you'll be able to move at close to full run speed without spending any stamina. Perfect for making long-distance runs quickly!

SONIC MANIA
BLUE THROUGH AND THROUGH

Sure, Tails can fly and Knuckles can glide, but nothing beats the thrill of mastering every stage in this retro-loving platformer using only Sonic. Keep your speed up and race to victory—you don't need those extra abilities to be a supersonic hero!

HOLLOW KNIGHT
BIG BAD BUGS

Sometimes, just beating a game isn't enough to say you're truly done with it, so you're going to have to get to *Hollow Knight*'s true ending if you want to claim mastery over it. How? We won't spoil that for you—just make sure you keep exploring!

TERRARIA
HOME IS WHERE THE START IS

Don't make your life easy by scouting out a good place for a camp. For a proper survival challenge, make your first load-in point your base of operations—and don't build any outposts further into the world. There's no place like home!

POWER UP!

THE DEFENSE RESTS

Take this one step further by not even allowing yourself to build any pits, moats, or other protective structures around your house. If you want to defend it, you'll have to get out there and do it yourself!

CHALLENGE TIME

TEKKEN 7

Treasure Battle mode grants better rewards the higher your win streak is. Can you take down over 20 opponents in a row and then beat one of the legendary challengers to claim their goodies?

SUPER MARIO PARTY

PARTY OVER HERE, OR ANYWHERE!

Grab a Joy-Con for the ultimate multiplayer mayhem! *Super Mario Party* gives the classic four-player party game a whole new twist thanks to the unique functions of Nintendo Switch.

There are more than 80 mini-games, including free-for-all, team battles, 3v1, and even all-new co-op. Each one makes good use of a wide range of the hardware, from motion controls to HD rumble. There's a party trick for every occasion!

Classic board games return with special dice for each character, while in the all-new River Survival mode, the four of you have to work together, rowing down a river with a number of branching paths and mini-games—can you make it to the end?

However you end up playing, don't forget to high-five each other!

QUICK TIPS!

SAVE UP COINS
On the board, coins can buy items or open certain paths. But don't forget that you need ten coins in order to get a star, so get saving!

MAKE SOME ALLIES
Having an ally means that you can use their character dice. They'll also boost your movement by one or two spaces.

BONUS STARS
It's not over yet. Bonus stars awarded at the end based on completely random things might just cause an upset.

TOP 5 MINI-GAMES

2 SIZZLING STAKES

It's a race to see who can cook all six sides of a delicious steak cube. Hold the Joy-Con vertically like it's a frying pan, and carefully try to flip your steak onto another side until it's all well done.

1 SLAPARAZZI

Who's going to get their best close-up? A camera sets up around the stage, and you'll want to get in the center for that perfect pose. And if anyone else gets in your way, push them aside!

3 NUT CASES

This 2v2 game makes rather clever use of HD rumble. Pick up each box, give it a shake, and feel the vibration to guess how many acorns are inside it. The team with the most acorns at the end wins!

4 OFF THE CHAIN

It's 3v1, or, rather, 1v3 in this case! One player rides the giant Chain Chomp around the arena, who charges straight at everyone else. Can the other team survive before time runs out, though?

5 NET WORTH

Each player is holding a corner of a fishing net, and you need to make sure you all shake your Joy-Con at the same time to lift the net to catch plenty of Cheep Cheeps. Don't miss the gold ones.

ALSO CHECK OUT ...

SUPER SMASH BROS. ULTIMATE
Pick your favorite gaming icon to fight in the ultimate mash-up.

OVERCOOKED! 2
This hilarious multiplayer game gives "food fight" a whole new meaning.

SUPER BOMBERMAN R
The classic couch multiplayer returns, supporting up to eight players.

GENT

Alright, alright. Someone's gotta fess up, or I've really come to my wit's end. I've searched high and I've searched low. I've gone through the art department, the break room . . . even that mangy finance guy's office. No dice.

Who ever thought that thing could go missing? Not me. Can't say I'm too beat up about it. But so long as it's out there, I gotta find it. What if it breaks? We can't have it leaking some-place it shouldn't be.

Do you know where this thing is? If you don't, I'll have to keep looking.

After all, the Ink Machine has to be here some-where . . . right?

Yours,
Thomas Connor

Thomas Connor

COMPANY SEEKS MISSING MACHINE

Evidence

BRIAR LABEL

BACON SOUP

BENDY

AIR 6 MAIL
CENTS
UNITED STATES OF AMERICA

HOW TO WIN AT APEX LEGENDS

GET THE W AND BECOME A LEGEND

THINK IN THREES

You should always be thinking about the fact that everyone is in squads of three. If you spot an enemy, assume there are two others nearby and attack accordingly. Attack as a team and outnumber opponents when possible—whoever gets the first down in a firefight has a huge advantage, as this puts you in a three-on-two situation.

STICK TOGETHER

In the early stages of a match, it's usually okay to spread out while you are focusing on collecting gear. However, as the game progresses you should stick relatively close to your teammates to make sure you're in a position to back each other up if you run into an enemy and are able to revive your buddies if they are downed.

5 BEST WEAPONS

We pick out the best weapons for taking out your enemies.

WINGMAN

It's not the easiest gun to use, but if you're good with it the Wingman is a fantastic handgun that uses heavy ammo. It's good at range and up-close you can hip-fire with it to devastating effect.

PEACEKEEPER

A low rate of fire means missing shots is a risk, but if you hit them you'll do heavy damage. With the choke attachment the Peacekeeper becomes even more dangerous, even at mid-range.

R-301

This gun is a great all-rounder and is relatively easy to use thanks to low recoil. With a few attachments —particularly an extended mag—it becomes even better.

R-99

This is a great gun, *if* you can find an extended magazine. Get hold of one of those and the gun's high rate of fire will make up for its low damage to make it into a very powerful option.

DEVOTION

This gun comes with some big downsides—energy ammo is quite rare, and it takes a little while to get going when you start firing. However, if you get the drop on an enemy and get it spun-up before they fire, it'll be incredibly effective.

FAST FACT

Apex Legends came out of nowhere: There was no promo material released until after the game's surprise launch.

DON'T REVIVE UNTIL IT'S SAFE

Never revive a teammate until you are sure it is safe. Enemies will be expecting you to come for your buddy and will be waiting for the opportunity to finish you off, too. Taking out the enemies that downed your teammate before you revive them is, more often than not, the best approach.

DON'T GIVE UP GOOD GROUND

There are times to rush opposing teams and there are times to stay put, so think about your position. If you're on high ground and in the circle, trading shots with a team outside the circle, why get drawn toward them? They will be forced to move when the circle closes in—then you can pick them off.

PICK A GOOD COMBO

Pick two weapons that complement each other. If you've got a sniper rifle, for example, make sure you also have a good short-range weapon for close-range encounters. It's also a good idea to pick weapons with differing ammo types, otherwise you're in danger of running out, though you can get away with it if you're using a sniper rifle—these single-shot weapons don't make much of a dent in your ammo reserves.

WATCH YOUR HEALTH

Keep a close eye on your health and know when to disengage from a combat encounter to heal up. Depending on the situation you're in, this isn't always possible, but it's a good idea to whenever you get the chance—taking a moment to heal up is better than getting downed and leaving your teammates outnumbered.

CLEAN UP

If you hear two teams fighting, try to get a view without getting involved. You can then sweep in when there are only a couple left or the fight is over to finish whoever is remaining before they get a chance to heal up.

GO ALL OUT

Don't worry about saving your abilities or grenades for later in the game, because there won't be a "later on" if you don't win the combat encounter in front of you. Go all out to wipe out a squad. You'll probably find your abilities will recharge in time for the next fight, and you can restock equipment from the crates that defeated players drop.

COMMUNICATE

Even if you're not on voice comms with your friends, *Apex Legends*' fantastic ping system makes it really easy to keep in touch with teammates. Tagging ammo they need, pinging attachments and armor that they can use, and spotting enemies is only going to make your team stronger and help you work together more effectively.

DON'T GET CAUGHT OUT

When you down an enemy, it's tempting to focus on finishing them off, but remember they are no threat while they are down, but their remaining teammates are. Keep an eye on the downed opponent to make sure they aren't revived, but focus your attention on their remaining squad members unless you're sure there are none close.

PICTURE THIS!

HOW TO IMPROVE YOUR LANDING

1 ASSIGN A MARKER

Prior to entering the Battle Bus, it's worth marking a landing spot on the map. This means you won't be wasting valuable time trying to identify a good area, allowing you to reach the ground as quickly as possible.

2 KEEP AN EYE ON THE MAP

In certain Limited Time Modes such as Blitz, the storm circle can appear before you land. It's always a good idea to watch your mini-map as a result. You might be able to switch direction at the last second.

3 LAND NEAR UNTOUCHED LOOT

Picking the right landing spot in *Fortnite* is crucial. Ideally, you want to strike a balance between a loot-filled and a relatively quiet location. Avoid busy areas such as Tilted Towers if you hope to evade lots of players.

4 WAIT TO LEAVE THE BUS

The majority of *Fortnite Battle Royale* players leave the Battle Bus instantly. As a result, it's always worth waiting a little longer before making the drop. Try avoiding the Battle Bus's path entirely to increase your odds of a quiet landing.

5 GLIDE TO YOUR TARGET

It's often believed that diving to your target is the quickest way to the ground. In actual fact, it's better to drop slightly before it, allowing you to float the rest of the way when your glider eventually opens.

THE LEGEND OF ZELDA

THE STORY CONTINUES

The Kingdom of Hyrule has seen some incredible events in its history. It's the home of Princess Zelda, Ganondorf, and Link, the Hero of Time. These three characters are locked in an ancient battle between good and evil, as Ganondorf tries to gather the Triforce, a mystical object that, when complete, gives the wielder huge power.

Thankfully, Link and the princess are there to stop him. There have been dozens of games in the *Zelda* series, as well as several spin-offs, each with its own clever ideas. Most recently, we saw the release of *Hyrule Warriors: Definitive Edition*. This fun action game brings characters from the whole *Zelda* series together in a unique story that's full of twists and turns.

QUICK TIPS!

AVOID CUCCOS
When you come across a chicken in Hyrule, don't attack it. If you do, it'll hit back—those beaks hurt.

GET THE SWORD
The Master Sword is the most powerful sword in the game. You can't beat Ganondorf without it!

LOCK ON
Hold the trigger on your controller and lock on to a nearby enemy. It makes it easier to attack.

TOP 5 ZELDA CHARACTERS

1 LINK

Who else would top our list? It's none other than the Hero of Time himself. Link is undoubtedly most famous for his green outfit. He wields the powerful Master Sword, which can lock away the evil power of Ganon.

2 PRINCESS ZELDA

Zelda isn't your typical princess. She wields a bow that fires magical arrows, and has a secret ninja alter ego named Sheik, who mysteriously appears to help Link in his quest.

3 TETRA

In *The Legend of Zelda: The Wind Waker*, a cartoony version of Link sails the sea to defeat Ganon. Along the way, he meets Petra, a no-nonsense pirate captain who helps in his quest. She looks familiar, though . . .

4 GANONDORF

Ganondorf was a member of the Gerudo race before he begins his quest to control the world. In some games, he transforms into a boar-like beast called Ganon. No matter his form, he's a dangerous foe.

5 LINKLE

In *Hyrule Warriors*, Linkle is a hero who believes she is the reincarnated Hero of Time. When the world is threatened, she sets out on a quest to save it. She wears a green cape similar to Link's outfit, and uses two crossbows.

ALSO CHECK OUT . . .

FINAL FANTASY XV
Another excellent fantasy adventure from the heavyweight series.

XENOBLADE CHRONICLES 2
Gather powerful blades in this action RPG.

SUPER SMASH BROS. ULTIMATE
All your favorite *Zelda* characters in one giant battle.

FIRE EMBLEM: THREE HOUSES

LEADING THE TROOPS

Three Houses brings a roster of new characters and a brand-new story (set in the land of Fódlan) to the Nintendo Switch. Of course, though it might have a new story, the game also has the fantastic turn-based tactical combat that the Fire Emblem series is known for. However, Fire Emblem: Three Houses also adds a cool, new twist that makes its combat stand out from previous games in the series. Each key character and the enemy generals you'll be going up against are flanked by a large group of troops on the battlefield. So, instead of going one-on-one against your opponents, you're leading your troops into battle against theirs, giving battles a more epic feel and tying into the game's story about the war.

QUICK TIPS!

BE CAUTIOUS
You don't get your characters back if they die during battle in Fire Emblem: Three Houses, so be careful when leading your troops into the fray. Plan your strategy carefully.

PLAN AHEAD
Think a few steps ahead when you are planning your moves so you don't place yourself in trouble.

STAY HEALTHY
It's a good idea to keep well stocked with health items so that you can always heal when needed. Planning ahead helps to prevent peril!

TOP ★★★ 5

FIRE EMBLEM CLASSICS

FIRE EMBLEM FATES: SPECIAL EDITION

Fire Emblem Fates was originally released as three separate versions: *Birthright*, *Conquest*, and *Revelation*. The *Special Edition* brings these three fantastic games into one package.

FIRE EMBLEM: AWAKENING

Perhaps the best thing about *Awakening* is that it offers the depth and challenge that the series is known for in its tactical combat. But it also does a great job of welcoming in players that are new to *Fire Emblem*.

FIRE EMBLEM

This entry on the Game Boy Advance was the first *Fire Emblem* game launched outside of Japan. It introduces us to this fantastic series, so it plays an important part in *Fire Emblem* history. Of course, it's a great game, too.

FIRE EMBLEM: RADIANT DAWN

How much you like *Radiant Dawn* will depend on how well you know *Fire Emblem*. It's not a good place to start for newcomers, but hardcore fans love it because of the game's tough challenge.

FIRE EMBLEM: PATH OF RADIANCE

Introducing 3-D to *Fire Emblem* on its release on GameCube, *Path of Radiance* still had the great gameplay, memorable characters, and emotional story that fans of the *Fire Emblem* series love.

ALSO CHECK OUT ...

DISGAEA 5
Another deep tactical game for lovers of strategy. Sixth game in its series.

VALKYRIA CHRONICLES REMASTERED
A remastered version of a strategy classic.

FINAL FANTASY VII
A simpler approach to turn-based combat for beginners in this classic RPG.

SPYRO REIGNITED TRILOGY

FAST FACT

Spyro is accompanied by a dragonfly friend called Sparx. The color of Sparx indicates how much health Spyro has.

BRINGING THE FIRE

Following the great success of the remastered *Crash Bandicoot* trilogy, Activision has decided to bring back another of its classic platforming characters from the era of the original PlayStation: the cute, purple dragon named Spyro. Spyro is best known today for his various appearances in the *Skylanders* games, but many are unaware that he once had his own series.

Spyro Reignited Trilogy reintroduces players to these classics, including updated versions of the first three *Spyro* games: *Spyro the Dragon*, *Spyro 2: Ripto's Rage!*, and *Spyro: Year of the Dragon*. In these three games, you will fight enemies, glide through the sky, meet a whole cast of colorful characters, and platform your way through a magical fantasy world, which is divided into realms for you to conquer.

QUICK TIPS!

FIRE PROOF
Bear in mind that your fire breath won't work on all enemies. Those with metal armor can block it.

RECOVERY
Don't forget that eating the butterflies that appear when you defeat small enemies will refill Spyro's health, so stock up.

HIDDEN TREASURE
Check behind every building and in every corner to find the gems that are hidden in every level.

A NEW LICK OF PAINT

OLD VS NEW
A lot of work has gone into updating the original PlayStation version of the game. From the mountains, to the lush green grass, to the balloon floating in the background, the remaster looks incredible.

SPYRO'S SKILLS
Spyro has a number of cool abilities. Being a dragon, he can, of course, breathe fire, but that's not all. Some levels even allow him to fly freely through the sky, while he is also able to glide.

MAGICAL WORLDS
This is Magic Crafters, which is one of the many worlds you can visit in *Spyro*. You travel between them through portals. Each world has a different look and theme, as well as some unique enemies and challenges.

DIVING DOWN
See that water down there? In the second *Spyro* game, *Ripto's Rage*, Spyro gains the ability to swim, enabling you to dive down and explore underwater areas and levels.

ALSO CHECK OUT ...

CRASH BANDICOOT N. SANE TRILOGY
The remastered platforming trilogy from *Spyro*'s first era.

SUPER MARIO ODYSSEY
If you love 3-D platforming, it really doesn't get much better than this.

ASTRO BOT RESCUE MISSION
Giving 3-D platforming a new dimension in the world of VR.

TOP 10 CO-OP GAMES

GREAT GAMES TO PLAY WITH FRIENDS

1 ROCK BAND 4

Everyone dreams about playing in a band, and this game makes it a reality. Pick any instrument you like—guitar, bass, drums, or a microphone—and choose from a large selection of on-disc songs or over a thousand DLC tunes. Add the optional *Rock Band Rivals* update into the mix, and you can even take the experience online.

2 POKÉMON: LET'S GO, PIKACHU! AND EEVEE!

Pokémon: Let's Go is the first game in the series to allow players to team up with a friend. Your partner can assist during battles and when catching Pokémon. And throwing Pokéballs at the same time will make them easier to catch!

3 GUACAMELEE! 2

This platform game enables you and up to three friends to compete as Mexican luchadores throughout a hand-crafted 2-D world. Players can drop in and out of the awesome adventure at any time, which features more enemies, moves, and a bigger map compared to the original game. Before long, you'll be pulling off jaw-dropping combos with your buddies!

4 MINECRAFT

Building worlds and fighting enemies in *Minecraft* is great on your own, but even better with friends. Whether playing locally or online across a variety of platforms, there are endless ways to team up and let your imaginations run wild. You can even take advantage of cross-platform support, which enables players to join each other's online servers on different devices.

5 FORTNITE

Epic Games's title has taken the world by storm in recent years, particularly in the case of its popular Battle Royale mode. You are able to play duos or squads in the latter, as you seek to become the last team standing, and it will take plenty of co-operation to emerge victorious. Alternatively, you could head into Creative or Playground mode together and go wild!

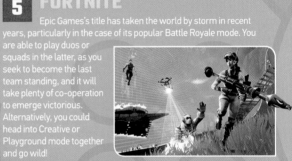

6 SEA OF THIEVES

Ahoy, mateys! Assemble your crew and then take to the seas in this fantastic pirate game from Rare. You will need to work as a team to discover *Sea of Thieves'* lucrative secrets, as well as compete against other players in destructive ship battles. Even during quiet times, there is something for every member of your crew to do, from buying cosmetic items to singing sea shanties.

FAST FACT

The arcade game *Fire Truck*, from 1978, is one of the earliest video games to feature a co-operative method of play.

EXPERT COMMENT
ROBIN VALENTINE
Games journalist

Overcooked! 2 **is the ultimate in organized chaos.** While preparing and serving the simple dishes with your friends seems easy at first, this co-op cooking game's succession of bizarre kitchens ramps up the pressure in no time, challenging you to make burgers across two speeding trucks, or boil soup in an earthquake. It'll test your friendships, too—if you can make it to the end of the level without yelling at each other about onions, then you're true friends!

7 CUPHEAD

Don't let *Cuphead*'s tough difficulty put you off playing, because it's both a beautiful and super-satisfying platformer to play. In co-op mode, two players can tackle the entire game as Cuphead and his pal, Mugman, working together to defeat various bosses. Don't expect to beat them straight away, however, because this game is all about learning from your mistakes, as you'll soon find out.

8 LEGO MARVEL SUPER HEROES 2

The first LEGO *Marvel Super Heroes* game was a smash hit back in 2013, but this sequel is both bigger and better. You can play the entire game in local two-player co-op, or take to four-player multiplayer in the new Battle Arena mode. There are loads of Marvel characters to choose from, too, including Spider-Man, Black Panther, and Groot.

OVERCOOKED! 2

10

This party game is all about creating complex meals in difficult settings. Work together to satisfy the requirements of your customers, taking on tasks such as cooking, cleaning, and chopping amid an array of bizarre scenarios. Expect plenty of hilarious moments and pressurized situations in this sequel, which is even better than the original game.

9 PORTAL 2

You've probably heard of this popular 2011 puzzle-platform game, but you might be surprised to hear of its terrific co-op mode. It's completely separate from the main game and tasks you and a friend with completing a series of test chambers. Expect plenty of tough challenges and satisfying solutions as you work to solve puzzles with portal guns.

3 TIPS FOR PLAYING AS A TEAM

Achieving success in co-op games is all about teamwork. Here are some tips to help:

PLAY LOCALLY WHEN YOU CAN

While playing online is a popular choice when embarking on co-op games, teaming up on the same console offers additional benefits. Not only does it improve communication in many cases, but it's also way more fun!

STAY CALM WHEN COMMUNICATING

The best way to achieve success when you're playing in co-op games is by remaining calm. That way, your voice and instructions will come across clearly to your teammates, enabling all of you to focus on the task without any confusion.

LEARN YOUR TEAMMATES' STRENGTHS

Each player on the team will boast different strengths in certain games. In *Fortnite*, for example, some players might be better at building than others. Take advantage of their skills to increase your chances of success.

10 OF THE BEST ROBLOX GAMES

THESE ARE THE GAMES YOU HAVE TO PLAY RIGHT NOW!

JAILBREAK

1 If there's one game you simply *must* play in *Roblox*, it's the brilliant fun of Jailbreak, which was an overnight success for teenage creator Alex Balfanz. You either play the role of a cop trying to stop the baddies or a criminal trying to cause trouble. It's really fun playing as a prisoner trying to make a sneaky escape from prison.

SPEED RUN 4

2 Speed Run 4 might have a simple name, but it's easily one of the most fun things to try in the world of *Roblox*. It's basically a time trial platformer where you'll need to run and jump across a course and try to complete it in the fastest time. It can get really tricky, so it's best to get some practice in before going for the best time.

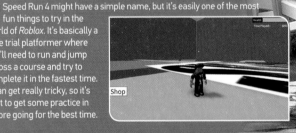

MAKE YOUR FIRST GAME!

Making your very first game in *Roblox* might seem scary, but you can do it!

SELECT A TEMPLATE

Once you open up Roblox Studio and start a new project, the first choice you'll need to make is what kind of terrain you'd like to use. This means the look, color, and feel of the land and sky that will make up your gameworld.

EDIT THE TERRAIN

Next, it's time to start doing some terraforming. This means changing how the land looks in your gameworld. You can smooth over hills, erode mountains to create spaces for hidden areas, and so much more. Start experimenting!

ADD SOME OBSTACLES

Now it's time to start adding in some obstacles. These can be all sorts of items you'd hope to find in your game. You can also group lots of objects together—this is known as a package, and it makes moving lots of objects much easier.

CUSTOM OBJECTS

Custom objects refers to special items that have been specially made for your game. These might be objects someone else made for you, or—once you've learned how to code—ones you've made yourself for your game.

UPLOAD YOUR CREATION!

When you're finished designing your gameworld you can publish it for other players to experience. Just select "Publish to Roblox" in the main edit menu and your creation will be uploaded. It's that easy!

BEE SWARM SIMULATOR

5 Okay, this is a weird one, but this is the joy of *Roblox*—you can pretty much do and make anything you like. And that includes creating a virtual swarm of bees. You can hatch bees, collect pollen, and make your own honey! Yes, it's very silly, but sometimes the best games involve the craziest ideas.

THEME PARK TYCOON 2

8 Taking inspiration from classic PC games such as *RollerCoaster Tycoon* and *Theme Park*—go and look them up, they're amazing—this *Roblox* version enables you to build your very own wonderland full of rides, amusements, and attractions. Earn money from your rides and build even more! You'll also need to make sure you keep the guests who visit your park happy.

MINING SIMULATOR

9 Mining Simulator is very similar to another blocky game about mining and crafting, but this is all about using different themes and styles as a backdrop for your world. From volcano-filled lava worlds to giant toy lands, this game is one of the most creative takes on *Roblox* ever. Get creative and unlock more themes.

WORK AT A PIZZA PLACE

3 It's time to join Builder Brothers Pizza parlor in one of the silliest and most enjoyable games in *Roblox*. As the name suggests, you'll be making and serving up those giant discs of Italian goodness with your friends. Other players will join the game and judge your efforts, so make sure you're on your best behavior!

MAD CITY

6 This game really lives up to its name. In this giant world you can play as a criminal causing trouble or a member of the local police trying to stop them. But that's not all. You can also take to the skies either as a supervillain causing havoc with your powers or by trying to stop all those naughty baddies as a superhero!

PET SIMULATOR

10 Unlike other simulators in *Roblox*, Pet Simulator is all about making your very own animal to play with and spend time with. You start out with either a cat or dog, but you can unlock new types of animals the longer you play. It's really cute, and your new furry companion will follow you wherever you go in the game!

ROBLOXIAN HIGH SCHOOL

4 Real-life school can be super boring, but that isn't the case in the land of *Roblox*. At Robloxian High School you won't have to go to any classes. Instead you get to hang out with all your friends and get an education in breakdancing, hang gliding, and more. It's still one of the most popular games in all of *Roblox*.

VEHICLE SIMULATOR

7 If you really love cars and things that go super fast, then Vehicle Simulator is the game for you. It features some of the best driving models in *Roblox*—this means each car drives in a more realistic way. It makes for some really fun car chases when you're playing as a criminal or as a member of the police.

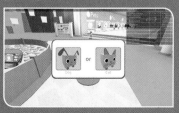

DREAMS
UNLEASH YOUR IMAGINATION

Dreams is part game, part creation tool. The idea is that you can make anything—sounds, music, characters, environments, objects, stories, art galleries, games—and mix and match those things as you wish. For example, you could make your own character and then create a scene where you use your DualShock 4 controller to animate the character like a puppet. Everything that you create can be shared with other people, too, so you are able to reuse each other's creations in the things that you are making. Otherwise, you can simply go and play through the creations that have been made by other people. There are limitless possibilities to what you can do with *Dreams* and so many different experiences for you to enjoy.

QUICK TIPS!

EXPLORE
Make sure you take some time out to actually enjoy the game and see what is possible, before jumping straight in to create yourself.

GET INSPIRED
See what other people are using *Dreams* to create, to see if that inspires any ideas in you.

REMIX
Remember that you don't have to create everything yourself in *Dreams*. You can grab characters and objects from other creators and use them in your own projects.

REALIZING YOUR CREATION

RESHAPE THE WORLD

Thanks to *Dreams*' creation tools, it's easy to make and reshape creations. You can sculpt them into new shapes, smudge edges, color in, copy and paste, and do just about anything else you can imagine.

PAINT THE LANDSCAPE

It's up to you whether you want to make a beautiful, painting-like landscape like this just to look at, or for people to play in. You could even find a landscape someone else has made and put it in your creation.

CHOOSE YOUR CHARACTERS

These characters look cute and cuddly, but you don't have to make creations like this. You can make simple creations, scary creations, funny creations . . . that freedom is what is great about *Dreams*.

DIFFERENT DIMENSIONS

Don't let this image fool you into thinking everything has to be in 3-D. *Dreams* is open to anything, so you could just as easily create a simple 2-D game, if that's what appeals to you.

ALSO CHECK OUT . . .

TEARAWAY UNFOLDED
Another from Media Molecule, *Tearaway* is a fun platformer with cool creation features.

MINECRAFT
If you love having the freedom to create, you can't go wrong with *Minecraft*.

CITIES: SKYLINES
Have fun building and managing your very own city in *Cities: Skylines*.

HOLLOW KNIGHT

INTO THE UNKNOWN

Hollow Knight takes place in a forgotten kingdom in a huge, underground world, full of secrets for you to uncover. You are let loose to explore that world, be amazed by its stunning locations, and find out more about the kingdom. Along the way, you must upgrade your character using the currency you collect by defeating enemies and by unlocking special abilities, such as the dash or double jump. Some of those abilities can only be earned by defeating one of the many cool bosses you can fight in the game. As well as meeting tricky enemies and bosses, you also come across friendly characters on your journey who can give you a helping hand, reveal new information about the world, or sell useful items.

QUICK TIPS!

CHARMING
Equip Charms that you find in the world to give your abilities a boost.

GET A MAP
In each area, you can find a map to buy. Make sure you do, because it will make exploration much easier.

DON'T GIVE UP
The early stages of the game are extra hard. Stick with it, improve your abilities, and you'll get into it.

TOP 5 ★★★

BOSSES

2 MANTIS LORDS

Sometimes one boss just isn't enough. You must defeat three when you take on the Mantis Lords—first, one by itself, and then two together. This fight requires some expert dodging for you to be successful.

1 NIGHTMARE KING GRIMM

Part of the free "Grimm Troupe" downloadable content, Nightmare King Grimm is a master class in boss design. It's a very challenging boss, but also feels fair, so it's super satisfying when you beat it. Grimm also has great music!

3 HORNET

This tough character is a real challenge to defeat in battle. You will come across her not once but twice during the game. Defeat her both times and she will help you out.

4 SOUL MASTER

You'll be punching the air when you win this epic fight. Until you realize that the Soul Master isn't quite done and comes back to battle you in a second phase. The second form is a bit easier.

5 DUNG DEFENDER

This big brute will throw balls of dung at you in order to take you down. At least he treats you much better once you have defeated him, though, and explains that it was all a bit of a misunderstanding.

ALSO CHECK OUT...

YOKU'S ISLAND EXPRESS
A fun, friendly Metroidvania.

ORI AND THE WILL OF THE WISPS
Tough with special abilities.

GUACAMELEE! 2
Another fantastic Metroidvania, but this one is far less serious.

COOLEST SECRETS

GREAT GAMES UNCOVERED

We love secrets in video games. They help create that feeling that you never quite know what you might see next, or what you might find if you investigate that little corner over there. The secret might just be a fun Easter egg referencing another great game. It could be a new character for you to unlock and play as, giving you a whole new way to experience a game you love. Or, it could be as big as a whole secret world that will test your gaming skills to their absolute maximum. Whichever it is, secrets are a great part of gaming, and we're going to show you some of our favorites . . .

DESTINY 2
THE FLOOR IS LAVA

Head to the upper walkway in the Tower and go to the water tanks. There you will get a "Don't Pick Me Up" prompt. Activate to trigger a "The Floor Is Lava" mini-game and finish it for a Quickness buff.

SEA OF THIEVES
HONORABLE MENTION

Check outside the tavern door at the Ancient Spire Outpost and you'll see a sign that says "LindsayElyse mind your head." This is a tribute to the Twitch streamer LindsayElyse, who fired herself from her cannon and landed perfectly in the doorway on her stream.

THE LEGEND OF ZELDA: BREATH OF THE WILD FIND THE MASTER SWORD

To get the powerful Master Sword you need to navigate your way through the mysterious Lost Woods. Follow the first path or torch lights until the end. Then, keep the wind blowing behind you and follow the path of the particles blowing in the air or light a torch and follow the path of the embers.

SUPER MARIO ODYSSEY
UNLOCK A SECRET KINGDOM

BEAT THE GAME

1 Your first goal should be to finish the game's main campaign by defeating Bowser.

BEAT THE DARK SIDE

2 The Odyssey still says it needs more moons. Collect 250 to unlock The Dark Side and defeat the five bosses you must fight there.

KEEP COLLECTING

3 Return to previous areas to get the moons left to collect. Five hundred will unlock The Darker Side, a secret kingdom for you to beat.

FORZA HORIZON 4
BARN CARS

As you play through *Forza Horizon 4*, hidden barns with cars inside will unlock. You can find one at Derwent Mansion. Exit the driveway, go straight on into the woods, and quickly turn left and you'll find the barn.

SUPER SMASH BROS.
ULTIMATE A HIDDEN HEART

Pause on the Great Bay level and select the camera controls. Zoom out and pan to the left to see a heart from Majora's Mask perched on the cliffs in the distance.

MARVEL'S SPIDER-MAN
CARD FROM THE DAREDEVIL

In one of Spider-Man's backpacks, you can find a Nelson & Murdock law office card. This is a reference to another Marvel hero: Daredevil. Select it in the inventory and Peter Parker will tell a story about a blind man giving him the card.

EXPERT COMMENT
MARIJAM DIDŽGALVYTĖ
Video games journalist writing for *The Guardian*, *Kotaku*, and more

Playing *Sims* during my teenage years was pure escapism—the limited budget offered in the game was bigger than my own family's. I would choose default houses and fill them with my friends. One day my brother told me about the dirty secret of "cheats"—codes you enter to get unlimited money. I enjoyed the game in such a mode for a while, building opulent residences with the latest gadgets for my Sims. Did it make us happier? Not really. Striving toward a goal is what brought bliss to the game—not soulless consumerism. When I knew the endgame, I couldn't enjoy it in the same way.

SUPER MARIO PARTY GOLDEN OAR
Complete all five routes in River Survival Mode and then head to the plaza. Talk to Birdo and she will offer you a golden oar as a reward for your skill.

MARIO KART 8 DELUXE GOLD MARIO
All characters are unlocked from the start in the Switch version of the game, apart from Gold Mario. Win all cups in the Grand Prix at 200cc to add him.

OVERWATCH ARCADE EASTER EGGS
On the Hanamura map, opposite the Rikimaru Ramen Shop, you will find an arcade. Look closely at the arcade cabinets and you will see they are packed full of references to other Blizzard games and even other retro franchises, such as *Metal Slug*.

NEW SUPER MARIO BROS. U DELUXE
FIVE-STAR FINISH

DEFEAT BOWSER

1 To get the first two stars of a five-star rating on your save file, defeat Bowser and beat every level, apart from Superstar Road.

COLLECT STAR COINS

2 Find every star coin in the game. You'll get a star for getting all the coins in Superstar Road 1–8 and one for the rest of the levels.

CAPTURE NABBITS

3 Capture all seven Nabbits and get every star coin in Superstar Road Level 9. Your save file will now have five stars.

SPYRO REIGNITED TRILOGY 99 LIVES

In the pause menu of the game you can enter cheat codes. Head into the menu and press R2, L2, R2, L2, Up, Up, Up, Up, Circle, and Spyro will get 99 lives. That should help you beat that tricky boss

CELESTE GAME IN A GAME

In Chapter 3, the Celestial Resort, you will go into a room where you find a note about the hotel closing. Look at the top of that room and you'll see a little nook. Climb up to access a secret area with a retro version of *Celeste* for you to play

OCTOPATH TRAVELER
SECRET SORCERER

To obtain the secret Sorcerer class, head to the Shrine of Archmagus in East Duskbarrow with a high-level party. At the end of the dungeon you can fight Dreisang the Archmagus. Beating him will unlock the Sorcerer class.

AWESOME CAMEOS

RUNBOW
SHOVEL KNIGHT

Perform the Butt Pound on ten enemies and you'll unlock Shovel Knight as a playable character.

SUPER TIME FORCE ULTRA
JOURNEY CHARACTER

On the PS4's *Super Time Force Ultra*, collect 25% of the Glorbs to unlock the main character from *Journey*.

SUPER SMASH BROS. ULTIMATE
VARIOUS

Grab an Assist Trophy and you'll be treated to cameos from a huge roster of stars including Akira from *Virtua Fighter* and the ghosts from *Pac-Man*.

SUPER MEAT BOY
COMMANDER VIDEO

On level 12, jump over Bandage Girl and enter the portal. You'll play mini-levels as Commander Video from the *Bit.Trip* series. When finished, he'll be unlocked.

HOLLOW KNIGHT
HIDDEN BOSS

To fight the Grey Prince Zote boss from the "Hidden Dreams" update, you first have to meet some conditions. You must save Bretta from the Fungal Wastes, save Zote from the Vengefly and again in Deepnest, then defeat him in the Colosseum of Fools. A trapdoor to the basement will open and you'll find a statue of Zote. Use the Dream Nail on it to start the Grey Prince Zote boss fight.

TOP 5 FORTNITE SECRETS

1 DISCO DANCING

Fortnite's dance emotes are part of its fame, so we love this dance-themed secret. At the Loot Lake Factory, if you and your friends dance on all four flowing tiles a disco ball rises from the floor.

2 COOL LOCATIONS

Fortnite is full of cool secret locations. We love the moon rocks you can find at the crash site post–Season 4 and the mansion on the island's east coast with a superhero base hidden in the basement . . .

3 A STRANGE PORTAL

When you dive into the map at the beginning of a game, try heading toward a small island southeast of Happy Hamlet. There you will find a small shack. Underneath the floorboards is a portal that will transport you back into the sky.

4 DOUBLE PUMP

Want to know an awesome secret that *Fortnite* doesn't tell you that will undoubtedly help your game? It's called the "double pump." Shotguns have a low firing speed, so grab two and quickly swap between them to fire shots at a faster speed.

5 TIP OF THE HAT

Look closely at the walls in *Fortnite* and you might spot a poster for a character called Jazz Jackrabbit. This is a cool Easter egg paying tribute to an old Epic (the same developer as *Fortnite*) game series, which started way back in 1994!

EXPERT COMMENT
JOHN RIBBINS
Developer at Roll7, creators of *Laser League* and *OlliOlli*

As a designer, I've always loved when video games have secrets. Personally, I like it when it feels more like a mystery than something only a couple of people will ever find. I think *Meat Boy* did this well with its portals and secret zones. They were always visible—the puzzle was figuring out how to get to them. It encouraged you to play the levels creatively and explore the whole map because there was the chance you'd find something cool tucked away that would pay off with a weird or wonderful bit of content.

DRAGON BALL FIGHTERZ
GOING SUPER SAIYAN

You can get some cool secret cutscenes in *Dragon Ball FighterZ* if you meet the right conditions. To get a scene that recreates the moment Goku first went Super Saiyan in the TV show, have Goku go up against Frieza on Planet Namek. Do not have Krillin on either team and you'll get a special intro. To finish with a special ending, defeat Frieza with a neutral heavy attack when he is the last fighter on his team.

GUACAMELEE 2!
GET THE HIDDEN ENDING

Find six hidden key pieces: one by playing through the story and the rest can be found in Templo de Jade, Isla Bonita, Infierno, and Los Manglares. Unlock the chicken temple door, complete the challenge, defeat the last boss.

FAR: LONE SAILS
TITANIC ACHIEVEMENT

Stand at the flagpole on the Landcruiser toward the end of the game to recreate the famous scene from the movie *Titanic* and you'll be rewarded with a hidden achievement for your acting skills!

MOONLIGHTER
SECRET SPARKLE

Keep your eyes open for a sparkle that appears around pits: They signify a hidden room. Roll into it and you will find some rare loot, a horde mode mini-game, a green chest, or, if you're unlucky, an empty room . . .

YOSHI'S CRAFTED WORLD
TIME FOR ARTS AND CRAFTS!

Yoshi's back for an all-new adventure on the Nintendo Switch. Everyone's favorite little green dinosaur is exploring his own hand-crafted world where he can flip between the front and back of game stages. An entire island of Yoshis are on hand, too—as well as his best pup, Poochy.

The Yoshi clan has to save their island's Sundream Stone from being stolen by Kamek and Baby Bowser. In the middle of a tussle, its gems fall off and scatter across various worlds. The Yoshis themselves are separated, too, so you'll have to find them all. There are plenty of cool secrets and fun unlockables to discover in Yoshi's cool, craft-centric world!

QUICK TIPS!

SUIT UP!
You can dress Yoshi in plenty of fun costumes to help him pass through each stage of the game.

FLIP IT!
When you're using the two-player co-op mode, have both players Ground Pound to swap between each level's perspective.

EGG THE ENEMIES
Toss some Yoshi eggs at enemies for a quick and easy solution to get them out of your way.

GET CRAFTING WITH YOSHI

FAST FACT

Many of the craft materials are made from product packaging, including *Mario Kart 8 Deluxe* "sponsors," such as Moo Moo Meadows Milk.

PAPERCRAFT PERIL

Everything in *Yoshi's Crafted World* is made out of regular, everyday household items like paper and cardboard. That means you might occasionally cross a bridge made of rolled-up paper or walk across strips of newspaper.

COLLECT 'EM ALL!

Yoshi's Crafted World is filled with flowers, coins, and Poochy Pups to collect as you explore each stage. Once you've finished one, you can play through it backward on the flip side to discover even more secrets!

BETTER WITH FRIENDS

Collect fellow Yoshis to help rescue everyone in each stage, because everyone needs a friend! You can even pass a Joy-Con to a friend to open up two-player co-operative play so you don't have to go it alone.

CREATIVE CRAFTING

There's a wide variety of stages to explore, whether you're checking out carefully arranged cardboard tubes or an entire area made out of delicious sweets. You never know what you'll see next when hanging out with Yoshi and friends.

ALSO CHECK OUT ...

POOCHY & YOSHI'S WOOLLY WORLD
Help Yoshi battle Baby Bowser!

YOSHI'S NEW ISLAND
As Yoshi, help Baby Mario rescue Baby Luigi.

SUPER MARIO MAKER
Create your own challenging *Super Mario* levels and games!

TOEJAM & EARL: BACK IN THE GROOVE

OLD SCHOOL IS BACK

The funky aliens that are ToeJam and Earl first entered the gaming world on the Sega Genesis back in 1991. Your goal was to explore the game's environment and collect the lost parts of your broken spaceship so the pair could leave Earth. The game's strange style and sense of humor won it a cult following, and now—all these years later—the duo is back. Like in the first game, you explore a series of floating islands, collecting objects while trying to avoid hostile enemies. While the game has a single-player mode, it also supports co-op play, so you can play with up to three friends either locally or online.

LEVEL 10

QUICK TIPS!

YOU GO THAT WAY

It's a good idea to split up from your co-op partner if you have one and head in different directions to uncover the map faster.

HEAL UP

Make sure you remember to keep an eye on your health bar. Don't forget to search for food when it gets low to fill it up again!

SNEAKY, SNEAKY

It's important that you don't wake up sleeping characters, especially as you can just sneak past them and avoid any trouble.

FEELING FUNKY

LEVEL 17

WIENER
4.00 ♥ 3

WIENER
2.00 ♥ 4

STRANGE STYLE
The game has the kind of fun, colorful, cartoony, and slightly strange style that made the original *ToeJam & Earl* a hit. Just why are those islands apparently floating in space?

GOTTA FIND FOOD!

COLLECTATHON
If you love collecting things, then this is the game for you. Right now, Earl could do with collecting some food to fill up his dangerously low health bar.

ON YOUR TOES
Characters like this riot shield–carrying cop are out to get you, so you can't simply explore without any pressure, and you've got to keep your guard up at all times.

SPLIT UP
When you and your co-op buddy are close, the game shows everything on one screen, but head in different directions and the game will go into split screen so that you can head off to explore on your own.

ALSO CHECK OUT . . .

SEGA GENESIS CLASSICS
A collection of classics from the console on which ToeJam and Earl made their debut.

PARAPPA THE RAPPER
Another game with a colorful character and hip-hop theme.

NEW SUPER MARIO BROS. U DELUXE
If you love collecting, there's plenty to find in this game.

THE BEST

MOBILE GAMES

Did you know that there are hundreds of thousands of mobile games available for iOS and Android? It's true! Trying to find the latest and greatest gems can be tough, but we're here to help. Here are 20 must-play games for smartphones and tablets, including both recent releases and enduring favorites . . .

STARDEW VALLEY

Lay down roots even when you're on the go! *Stardew Valley* lets you run your own farm as you please, all while building relationships, restoring the town, and doing plenty more.

· 20 ·

KINGDOM RUSH VENGEANCE

· 19 ·

Mobile's best tower defense series is back! This time you control the bad guys—but you still drop down an array of towers to defeat foes.

ODDMAR

This gorgeous, side-scrolling Viking quest looks like a cartoon in motion, but it's much more than that: It's a challenging platform-action game that plays perfectly even without a gamepad in hand.

18

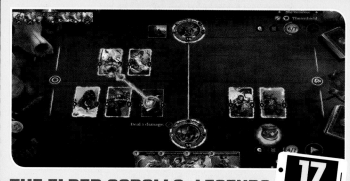

17

THE ELDER SCROLLS: LEGENDS

Bethesda's beloved *Elder Scrolls* role-playing franchise comes to life in a very different way in *Legends*, a turn-based card-battler that's a lot like *Hearthstone*. Even so, the mix of familiar characters and sights and various tactical tweaks makes *Legends* very compelling on its own.

GOROGOA

This is an incredibly clever puzzle game which finds you exploring a series of images and layering them on top of each other to discover unexpected solutions. It's truly mesmerizing stuff and is a great way to kill time on the bus, train, or plane . . .

16

15

FINAL FANTASY XV: POCKET EDITION

It's the same core, epic role-playing quest as on consoles, but *Final Fantasy XV: Pocket Edition* has been streamlined and rebuilt for phones and tablets. The newly cartoonish look is charming and you still embark on a captivating adventure with compelling heroes.

POCKET CITY

Pocket City is the best *SimCity*-esque simulation built for mobile to date. It very easily allows you to slap down roads, houses, and buildings with your finger and expand the little city with ease and the minimum of effort!

14

ANIMAL CROSSING: POCKET CAMP

13

This is definitely the most adorable time suck that you could possibly find on mobile. Nintendo's popular console franchise is a perfect fit for smartphones, as *Pocket Camp* lets you build up and customize your own little campground as you explore the island, play fun mini-games, and interact with the local animal inhabitants.

FAST FACT

Final Fantasy XV: Pocket Edition has since been ported back to consoles and PC, so PS4, Xbox One, and PC owners can play either version of the game.

12

CLASH ROYALE

Still one of the best competitive experiences on mobile, *Clash Royale* lets you take a deck of fantasy-themed warrior cards into battle and use them to destroy the rival castle while defending your own. Madness!

11

BENDY AND THE INK MACHINE

The kid-friendly horror hit is just as eerie and captivating on mobile, as *Bendy and the Ink Machine* sees you explore an abandoned animation studio while evading the freaky ink-based scares within.

ARENA OF VALOR

Arena of Valor brings the same kind of in-depth MOBA experience to touch devices, with electrifying 5v5 battles in which each team of heroes tries to topple the enemy's base. It's streamlined for mobile play, but still packs in loads of tactical strategy.

10

9

DONUT COUNTY

This strange and delightful little game sees you controlling an ever-growing sinkhole that is opening up in the ground as you suck up the local terrain and solve puzzles along the way. It's incredibly cute and charming. Mmm . . . donuts.

8

POCKET-RUN POOL

Pocket-Run Pool turns the classic game of table billiards into a speedy arcade challenge. In this version of the game, you need to shoot for the top score by sinking balls into specific pockets without "scratching" the cue ball.

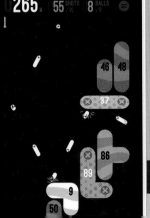

HOLEDOWN

Dig deeper and deeper into the surface of the planet in *Holedown*. You can launch up to a staggering 99 balls at a time to clear all of the obstacles below. It's very simple and very smart, but also very chaotic!

7

ALTO'S ODYSSEY

Shred some sand in the gorgeous *Alto's Odyssey*, which shifts away from the snowy slopes of *Alto's Adventure* while keeping the engaging, low-key vibe. Grind on ropes, grab some air, bounce off of the water, and take in the game's dazzling sights.

ASPHALT 9: LEGENDS

You won't find a more thrilling racer on mobile. *Asphalt 9: Legends* lets you command an array of licensed rides as you bash rivals and grab serious air en route to a first-place finish.

MINECRAFT

Is there anything else to say about the game that took over the planet? It's still amazing that you can get a robust, fully fledged *Minecraft* experience wherever you are. The mobile edition lets you create, battle for survival, and collaborate online with buddies.

POKÉMON GO

Pokémon GO keeps getting better and better, as Nintendo's location-based catch-'em-all experience now has hundreds of monsters to find along with head-to-head battles, Pokémon trading, fun community events, and plenty more.

FORTNITE

Not sitting in front of your console or PC? You can still play *Fortnite* on your phone or tablet and it's the very same battle royale experience. Shoot and build to survive the 100-player brawl and see if you can secure the Victory Royale.

BRAWL STARS

Brawl Stars is part battle royale, part objective-based team shooter, and even part soccer! The rapid-fire matches are short but deeply entertaining, as you work with allies to capture gems or survive a battle royale gauntlet—either on your own or with a buddy in tow. Difficult to put down!

FAST FACT

Brawl Stars spent more than 500 days "soft launched" in certain countries and was greatly enhanced before the full worldwide release.

KINGDOM HEARTS III
THE KEY(BLADE) TO YOUR HEART

The thrilling conclusion to the main *Kingdom Hearts* story unravels in *Kingdom Hearts III*. The game follows hero Sora and his team—including Goofy, Donald Duck, King Mickey, and a ton of your favorite Disney characters—as they look to prevent another Keyblade War. This chapter in the series introduces new game worlds like *Frozen*, *Tangled*, and *Toy Story*. There are also some new character summons called "Links" that come with Keyblade transformations. Fans have plenty to discover in the game as they meet new Square Enix and Disney friends, interact with old pals, and figure out how to stop the villainous Xehanort from fulfilling his evil plans. A grand adventure for all, and a thrilling end to a long-running series.

QUICK TIPS!

EXPLORE THE OTHER KINGDOM HEARTS
Kingdom Hearts is a series packed with story and memorable characters—check out the rest of the games.

DON'T HOARD ITEMS
Don't stockpile items and power-ups! Use them freely in the heat of battle to help yourself and your squad.

PAY CLOSE ATTENTION TO THE STORY
Kingdom Hearts III is packed with twisting plot points. Make sure you're paying attention!

SIMPLE AND CLEAN

USE A DAZZLING ATTACK ARSENAL

Use some totally awesome attacks that correspond to the themed worlds you're exploring. While hanging out with the *Monsters, Inc.*, crew, transform into a cool monster form and let some devastating abilities loose!

MEET YOUR FAVORITE DISNEY CHARACTERS

Sora, Donald, and Goofy are meeting up with your favorite Disney characters once more, from *Tangled*'s Rapunzel to *Frozen*'s Elsa and plenty of others. Help them complete missions with special themed attacks and fun objectives to explore.

SUMMON DISNEY CHARACTERS IN BATTLE

Send for iconic Disney characters like Ariel, Simba, Wreck-It Ralph, and Stitch in the heat of battle to push combat to the next level. They're here to help—all you have to do is call them forth!

SEE THE END OF KINGDOM HEARTS

Follow the long-running *Kingdom Hearts* story to its thrilling conclusion at long last. *Kingdom Hearts III* wraps up an extremely long and complicated story, and you won't want to miss out on the way it all ends.

ALSO CHECK OUT . . .

KINGDOM HEARTS: THE STORY SO FAR
Get up to speed with the *Kingdom Hearts* universe.

WORLD OF FINAL FANTASY
Final Fantasy meets *Pokémon* in this adorable adventure.

NI NO KUNI II: REVENANT KINGDOM
Take the throne and rule over your own kingdom!

FAST FACT

The game's graphics are "HD 2-D," a beautiful combination of classic character sprites with modern lighting and effects.

OCTOPATH TRAVELER

AN EIGHT-OF-A-KIND ADVENTURE

An epic journey inspired by classic RPGs, *Octopath Traveler* casts you in the role of eight different adventurers. There's the knight Olberic, the dancer Primrose, the apothecary Alfyn, the hunter H'aanit, the scholar Cyrus, the cleric Ophilia, the thief Therion, and the merchant Tressa.

Choose whoever you want at the start. Your paths will intertwine as each traveler joins your adventure, and you get to explore in full each and every character's rich story. Explore an open map filled with towns, deadly dungeons, and exciting battles with the game's unique turn-based system.

QUICK TIPS!

PATH ABILITIES
Each character has a unique Path Ability to get past obstacles or access items. Therion is especially good at stealing items!

RECRUIT COMPANIONS
Both Primrose and Ophilia can recruit other characters in towns. Tressa can even spend money on hired help!

GET ANOTHER JOB
Search for shrines hidden in the world. They unlock jobs, letting characters learn to use another character's weapons and skills.

BATTLE BOOST BREAKDOWN

TIMELINE MANAGEMENT

The timeline at the top shows the order of each character's turn in battle. The trick is to disrupt this order. With the right ability or attack you can delay or cancel an enemy's turn or give your party a head start.

BOOST POINTS

Each turn, your character gains a Boost Point (BP). Spending BP can let you use the same attack multiple times or make abilities like spells or buffs more powerful. Use BP wisely to give your party the edge!

Thousand Spears

Olberic
HP 2.364 / 2.364
SP 50 / 111

Tressa
HP 1.139 / 2.447
SP 90 / 95

Therion
HP 1.787 / 2.155
SP 76 / 82

H'aanit
HP 2.166 / 2.166
SP 84 / 92

WEAK
169
WEAK
167
VULNERABLE
169
VULNERABLE
VULNERABLE

FINDING AND EXPLOITING WEAKNESSES

Every enemy has weaknesses against certain weapons or elements. Once you find out what's effective, keep exploiting the attacks. Breaking an enemy's shield not only cancels their turn, but they'll take twice as much damage from your attacks!

PARTY ROTATION

You might have eight travelers in total, but only four can fight at a time. Each has their own unique strengths and abilities, so you'll want to change your roster from time to time. It's also important to keep everyone leveled up!

ALSO CHECK OUT . . .

BRAVELY DEFAULT
A handheld epic with tons of jobs and fantastic battles to keep you busy.

XENOBLADE CHRONICLES 2
A huge, sprawling RPG with a deep battle system.

TALES OF VESPERIA
An RPG with fighting-game battles and wonderful anime characters.

10 OF THE BEST BATTLE ROYALE ITEMS

KEEP AN EYE OUT FOR THESE ITEMS ON THE MAP

1. ASSAULT RIFLE

The Assault Rifle has long been the weapon of choice for many *Fortnite* players, and there are many variations of it to collect. The Heavy Assault Rifle deals more damage than the standard version, while the Thermal Scoped Assault Rifle allows you to see through buildings, helping you to spot hiding players.

2. SHIELD POTION

An important consideration in *Battle Royale* is to collect Small Shield Potions. These increase your health by 25% every time and can be consumed quickly. Harder-to-find standard Shield Potions offer a 50% boost and you might even find a Chug Jug if you're lucky, filling up your health and potion meters.

3. ROCKET LAUNCHER

The Rocket Launcher is an extremely powerful tool in the right circumstances, but in close-range scenarios, it can actually prove more troublesome than it's worth. Instead, try to save this rare item for the latter stages of a game (particularly in Solo, Duos, and Squads), where it can be used to destroy bases and bring players out of hiding.

4. BANDAGES

Healing is an important part of *Battle Royale*, and while Med Kits can restore you to full health, Bandages are actually more beneficial to carry around. This is because they are far quicker to apply and can restore 15 times health each time (up to 75%). You don't want to be wasting time when opponents are nearby, so keep this in mind.

5. PUMP SHOTGUN

Whether you choose to prioritize the Pump or Tactical Shotgun is up to you, but the former is more powerful. It's best used for close-range scenarios, such as 1v1 battles, and requires a surprising amount of accuracy to use well. The rare Heavy Shotgun is also a great option and can often be found in supply drops.

6. PORT-A-FORTRESS

It's time-consuming and a drain on your resources to build bases, making the Port-a-Fortress very useful . As the name suggests, you can use it to summon a giant fortress, complete with Bouncers for a quick getaway. A great way of getting the high ground over your competitors, particularly in later stages.

9. GRENADE LAUNCHER

Much like the Rocket Launcher, this item is best saved for the end of a match. It's important to be precise with the Grenade Launcher, as aiming it directly at players and structures will see your grenades bounce harmlessly away. This rare item is most effective when aiming it into the open ceilings and walls of enemy bases.

FAST FACT

French soccer player Antoine Griezmann celebrated his goal in the 2018 FIFA World Cup final by performing the *Fortnite* move "Take the L" dance.

7. SNIPER RIFLE

The best method for getting long-range eliminations is with the Sniper Rifle. You can increase your chances by opting for variants such as the Heavy Sniper Rifle, which offers more damage than the standard version. Don't forget to aim higher than usual when standing at a particularly long range, due to the amount of distance involved.

8. DAMAGE TRAP

This item offers a great method for tricking your opponents, activating a spiky trap toward anyone who approaches it. As a result, it's a good idea to hide the item in ceilings, trapping unsuspecting players as they enter buildings. It's also a great way to eliminate players who are following you, but only if you're stealthy about it!

10. RIFT-TO-GO

There are many reasons why you might need the Rift-To-Go, which throws you back into the air for a soft landing. Primarily, it's used to readjust your position, such as when fleeing the storm or getting out of a tough spot. It's worth having one in your inventory, because you never know when you might need it.

5 WAYS TO GET A VICTORY ROYALE

The best tips you need to emerge victorious in Solo, Duos, and Squads . . .

LEARN TO BUILD QUICKLY

Building is a key part of *Fortnite Battle Royale*— it's an important tool for designing bases, protective walls, and ramps. It's hard to get a grasp on it. If you're struggling, practice making structures in Playground.

ALWAYS COVER YOUR BACK

With 99 other players on the map, anyone could be watching you. When you're remaining stationary, such as searching supply drops and healing, build a wall around you for protection.

STICK TO THE CIRCLE'S EDGE

Play smart to guarantee a top-ten finish, following the border of the storm circle to avoid others. This tactic is even more effective at the map's edge, but make sure you loot up first.

JUMP TO AVOID BEING HIT

You'll notice players jumping around the map as they run. This is to avoid stray shots, making their movements unpredictable. Get into the habit of doing this, and you're less likely to be hit from afar.

WORK TOGETHER AS A TEAM

It's important to work as a team. Think outside the box—approach opposing players from various angles, use different weapons, and never leave your teammates' side for long.

ULTIMATE ACHIEVEMENTS

If you're a hardcore gamer, chances are you love chasing achievements. But no matter how great you are at a particular game, there are some out there that are incredibly, ridiculously difficult to win. They push you to continually improve yourself until you can finally get them. It'll be frustrating along the way but it's worth it in the end . . .

1

N++
[PS4]

Platinum

Snagging this trophy is all about getting perfect scores in every single level of *N++*, so be prepared to put in a lot of time if you want to get your hands on this one—you'll be handsomely rewarded!

2

ROCK BAND 2
[XBOX 360, PS3]

The Bladder of Steel Award

This achievement requires you to do exactly what it sounds like—"hold it" for a very long time! You have to complete the game's "Endless Setlist 2" and play for around six to seven hours without cheating, stopping, or failing!

3

MEGA MAN 10
[PS4, XBOX ONE, SWITCH, PC]

Mr. Perfect

Mega Man 10 can be an impossible game to beat for those who aren't totally dedicated, but when you can't get hit even once? That's even worse! That's what you're required to do for Mr. Perfect—good luck with it . . .

Dr. Wily
I've simply come to give Dr. Light a message!

4

CUPHEAD
[PS4, XBOX ONE]

Beat The Devil at His Own Game

This is an extremely tough one. You've got to beat *Cuphead* on Expert, which means you first have to beat it on Normal. That can be extremely hard—especially if you have difficulty winning on the first playthrough!

TOP 5 EASIEST ACHIEVEMENTS

PRESS START TO PLAY

THE SIMPSONS GAME

The name of the achievement says it all. Just press start and you'll nab this incredibly easy reward. What are you waiting for?

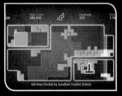

FAIRY GODMOTHER

CHIME

This achievement will unlock as soon as you load up *Chime*. If that sounds ridiculously simple, well, it is.

USED LEO'S SPECIAL MOVE

TMNT

All you need to do to bag this achievement is play as the character Leo, then press a button to use his special move.

WHERE'S THAT TEMPLE?

PRINCE OF PERSIA

Start *Prince of Persia*, meet the character Elika, then talk to her to discuss your next moves. Bam! Achievement unlocked.

THE FLOW OF COMBAT

AVATAR: THE LAST AIRBENDER: THE BURNING EARTH

Want to make an insanely easy 1,000 score? Keep tapping attack. Seriously. That's it.

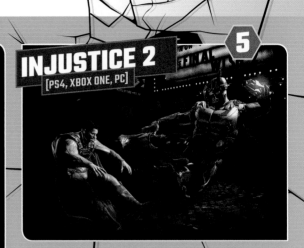

INJUSTICE 2
[PS4, XBOX ONE, PC]

5

Cat Fight

This achievement isn't so bad in practice: You have to defeat Cheetah using Catwoman's Cat Call ability. But getting Cat Call is only possible through unlocking Mother Boxes—which are all random. Happy hunting, you'll get there eventually!

TITAN SOULS
[PC]

6

Iron Mode

Titan Souls is an extremely difficult game as it is, but slaying all of the game's Titans in Iron Mode takes a particularly talented player. Therefore, it's one of the hardest achievements you will find. Can you slay 'em all?

7

TETRIS EFFECT
[PS4]

Serious? Seriously

Tetris Effect can be an extremely difficult game, and this achievement asks that you score an SS rank everywhere you possibly can. Good luck, you're gonna need it—especially if you're not a natural at *Tetris*.

8

OVERCOOKED!
[PS4, XBOX ONE, SWITCH, PC]

All the Trimmings

Overcooked! makes it extremely difficult to serve up the perfect food to your customers as it is, but this achievement wants you to get the perfect score of three stars per kitchen! Crazy, right?

9

CLOUDBERRY KINGDOM
[XBOX 360]

Shenanigans!

This achievement may sound relatively simple, but it means you need to complete Chapter 7, which is arguably one of the hardest ones in the entire game. There's so much going on you hardly have time to breathe!

FORTNITE
[PS4, XBOX ONE, SWITCH, PC]

10

Talented Builder

Think that you play a lot of *Fortnite*? This achievement knows better. Talented Builder has you building 500,000 structures. Imagine just how many things you build in a normal *Fortnite* match and you can start to realize just how ridiculously difficult this is to obtain.

OVERWATCH
[PS4, XBOX ONE, PC]

11

The Floor Is Lava

The Floor Is Lava is one of the toughest achievements to unlock in *Overwatch*, period, even if you're an expert Lucio player. You've got to get three kills while riding on walls without dying while playing Quick or Competitive Play.

FAST FACT

Some video games feature their own in-game achievements separate from the ones you earn on your console or PC.

SPEEDRUNNERS
[PS4, XBOX ONE, PC]

12

The King of New Rush City

Speedrunning is hard enough to do in any game, but a whole game dedicated to it is even more crazy. To get this achievement, you've got to beat every chapter in the game on the Unfair difficulty.

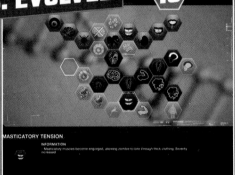

13

LITTLE NIGHTMARES
[PS4, XBOX ONE, SWITCH, PC]

Hard to the Core

Hard to the Core has you racing to complete the terrifying game *Little Nightmares* in under an hour without dying once. It's not too hard to not die, but the time pressure makes this a tough one.

14

RUNBOW
[PS4, XBOX ONE, SWITCH, PC]

Indigestible

This 2-D platformer is cute and colorful, but it's extremely challenging, especially if you're tackling the Indigestible achievement. Beat the Bowhemoth in ten deaths or under 20 minutes and it's yours. Sound simple? Good luck—it's not.

PLAGUE INC. EVOLVED
[PS4, XBOX ONE, PC]

15

Power Overwhelming

This weird achievement requires that you turn specific people in the world into vampires and then let them "consume the bones at Stonehenge," which makes little sense. There's so much that goes into getting it that it would make your head spin.

MASTICATORY TENSION

INFORMATION
Masticatory muscles become engorged, allowing zombie to bite through thick clothing. Severity increased

DNA 6   INFECTIVITY   SEVERITY

16

LEGO WORLDS
[PS4, XBOX ONE, SWITCH, PC]

Billionaire!

The sandbox adventure game LEGO *Worlds* is an exciting alternative to *Minecraft*, but this achievement is a doozy. It asks you to collect a billion studs, which is going to take quite some time.

I AM BREAD
[PS4, XBOX ONE, PC]

17

Turophile

You control a simple piece of bread in this simulation game and this achievement asks you to step up your game considerably. It wants you to get an A++ rating on all Cheese Hunt levels, where you find and collect pieces of cheese.

18

THE GOLF CLUB 2
[PS4, PC]

Millionaire

Playing golf should be peaceful, right? Not when you're trying to earn a net worth of a million dollars in *The Golf Club 2*. Prepare to spend quite a bit of time reaching your goal.

EXPERT COMMENT
RAY NARVAEZ JR.
Full-time streamer and achievement hunter

Achievement hunting is a niche hobby that requires both dedication and persistence. I have been achievement hunting for almost 15 years. Often achievements are time-consuming, challenging, and/or tedious. One of the hardest achievements I've unlocked is Fector's Challenge in *Stardew Valley*, which requires you to "Beat 'Journey of the Prairie King' without dying." This single achievement is not only challenging but very luck-dependent, so much so that less than 1% of people who have played the game on Xbox have unlocked it.

FINAL FANTASY VII
[PS4, XBOX ONE, SWITCH, PC]

Materia Overlord

There are over 50 different types of Materia magic in *Final Fantasy VII*, and for this achievement you have to spend hours mastering every single one. Some of them even require that you earn every skill in the game.

Tera Flare

NAME — Cloud | BARRIER | HP 4505/5000 | MP 999 | LIMIT | TIME

19

FAST FACT

There are various websites online that you can use to track achievement and trophy stats for gamers worldwide. Join up and get involved!

20

GARRY'S MOD
[PC]

Yes, I Am the Real Garry!

You may never get this achievement, not in a million years. You've got to be in the right place at the right time for this once-in-a-lifetime achievement. You have to connect to the same game server that developer Garry Newman is on so you can play together at the same time. There's a huge catch, though—he's hardly ever online. If you manage to bag this achievement, consider yourself a unicorn among Steam gamers.

PICTURE THIS!

GET TO KNOW SUPER SMASH BROS. ULTIMATE

STAGE HAZARDS

Every stage has its own hazard
be turned off in the settings. Th
be something as simple as a pa
stage disappearing during the
it could be a character entering
attacking the stage.

STAY IN THE ARENA

Luring enemies toward the end of a
stage in the hope of eliminating them is a
risky move. We recommend weakening
the opponent, making them easier to
launch out of the arena, then hitting
them with a strong attack.

YOUR PERCENTAGE

Keep your eye on this number—the
higher it gets, the more likely you are
to be knocked out of the arena. Try to
find healing items to lower your
percentage, but be careful as some
items may do more harm than good.

32.2%
MARIO

56.0%
JIGGLYPUFF

KNOW YOUR ABILITIES

There are over 70 different playable characters, each with their own moveset. The game has a Training mode that let's you practice attacks on an unmoving target. Use this to work on combos that you can use in competitive games.

20.0%
SHULK

LIMIT

56.0% FF
CLOUD

LUMINES REMASTERED

ABOLISH BLOCKS TO THE BEAT

Lumines is like a hyperactive, sugar-fueled *Tetris*. Yes, it's a puzzle game about rotating and matching little chunks of blocks, but there's so much more going on here. Your goal is to match and clear groups of like-colored blocks, but you'll earn way more points if you amass huge stacks of them and build combos to maximize the BPM (beats per minute) bar that scrolls across the screen. What's that all about, we can hear you ask. Well, the gameplay in *Lumines* is tied to the beat of the music with each new audio/visual skin that's draped atop the screen, which changes the feel and flow of the action. This remastered edition of *Lumines* updates the original 2005 game with crisper graphics, letting you enjoy one of gaming's greatest puzzlers all over again.

QUICK TIPS!

KEEP CLEAR

Early on, do your best to keep the board relatively empty. Clear blocks quickly to leave plenty of space—and avoid stacking upward.

ADD RAPIDLY

Once you have a 2x2 square ready to be cleared, quickly drop additional like-colored blocks on it to create more squares before the BPM bar arrives.

CHAIN 'EM ALL

The glowing chain block will clear any like-colored blocks that it touches, so position it perfectly to erase a huge mass in one move.

HOW LUMINES WORKS

THE BPM BAR

This yellow line moves left to right at the same pace as the music and it'll remove any blocks that are added on to a completed square. Slower songs provide more time to create even larger combinations.

THE BLOCKS

Each cluster is a 2x2 square that you can quickly rotate in either direction and move left or right to find the ideal destination. The goal is to create a single-color square below, then add more blocks to clear them all at once.

SCORE x4

TIME 25

11:43

SCORE 000640

118,685

HI-SCORE

118,685

DELETED

515

YOUR AVATAR

You can add a personalized touch to the game by choosing one of 44 unlockable avatars that hover in the bottom left of the screen. You can be a girl or a boy, a dog or a bunny, or even a block of cheese.

THE SKIN

Lumines Remastered features more than 40 different skins, each of which features a unique background, varying block colors or textures, and a backing song. Each skin is wildly different from the others and alters the tone of the game.

ALSO CHECK OUT...

TETRIS EFFECT
Tetris gets a dreamy makeover on PS4 from the creator of *Lumines*.

SUSHI STRIKER: THE WAY OF SUSHIDO
Nintendo's original Switch and 3DS game is a quirky puzzler.

REZ INFINITE
Explore the pulsing world inside a computer in this euphoric gem.

THE BEST

PLAYSTATION NOW

& XBOX GAME PASS

GAMES

Whether you're an Xbox or PlayStation fan, a subscription service is a great way to access hundreds of games for a monthly fee. Separating the best from the worst can prove difficult, however, so here are some particularly fun titles available through PlayStation Now and Xbox Game Pass.

BROTHERS: A TALE OF TWO SONS 20

This unique adventure game requires you to control two brothers on your controller. You'll require the brothers' skills to complete various puzzles throughout the story.

GRIP: COMBAT RACING 19

This high-octane racer features multiple courses, vehicles, and weapons. The cars can actually defy gravity, allowing them to drive up walls and across ceilings.

SCREAMRIDE

If you're a thrill-seeker, this one's for you! *ScreamRide* is all about creating amazing roller coasters, riding them at high speeds, and even destroying them via the brilliant Demolition Expert mode.

18

17

RATCHET & CLANK: A CRACK IN TIME

You'll find this much-loved PS3 game on the PlayStation Now service. Although ten years old, this platformer remains one of the best games in the series to date. Don't forget to check out additional *Ratchet & Clank* titles on PS Now, too.

LEGO STAR WARS: THE COMPLETE SAGA

LEGO games can be found on both subscription services, but this one is particularly special—two full games, six *Star Wars* episodes, and even online-co-op support are crammed into it.

15

STEEP

Fans of extreme sports need look no further than Ubisoft's massive open-world game, which allows you to try skiing, snowboarding, paragliding, and wingsuit flying across various locations. There's also DLC that lets you compete in the Winter Olympics!

16

HUMAN: FALL FLAT

An open-ended physics-based puzzle game, *Human Fall Flat* tasks you with overcoming numerous obstacles as the character Bob. The awkward controls make this game hilarious to play—or even to just watch!

14

13

ORI AND THE BLIND FOREST

This charming and gorgeous-looking 2-D platformer was a big hit when it was released, winning Xbox Game of the Year at the 2015 Golden Joystick Awards. In the game, you control a Guardian Spirit named Ori through a selection of brilliantly designed puzzle levels. Try it on Xbox Game Pass.

12

BROKEN AGE

Point-and-click game *Broken Age* is a challenging puzzle adventure based around the stories of two teenagers. It boasts a selection of famous voice actors including Elijah Wood, Masasa Moyo, and Jack Black.

OLLIOLLI2: WELCOME TO OLLIWOOD

There haven't been many truly great skateboarding games in recent years, but 2-D game *OlliOlli* and its sequel are definite exceptions. If you love the sport, these are for you.

11

KNACK

This third-person platforming game features a lead character who can grow dramatically bigger in size as he collects relics. *Knack* was developed as a launch title for the PS4 and was directed by legendary games designer, programmer, and producer Mark Cerny.

10

x19   Bluntslide

9

PES 2019

FIFA's biggest rival continues to play a great game of soccer, complete with various modes including Master League, Become a Legend, and myClub. New features in *PES 2019* include improved graphics, Visible Fatigue, and a huge set of new licenses.

8

ONRUSH

Although *Onrush* looks like a racing game, it's actually a team-based arcade-style vehicular combat title with plenty of unique features and cool modes. A great one to play with friends, you can play with up to 12 (in two teams of six).

7

JOURNEY

Not the terrible soft rock band that your dad listened to in the 1980s, but a game first released in 2012 on the PS3. It's a super calm, beautiful indie title that sees you guiding a mysterious figure on a breathtaking journey.

THE BEST PS NOW AND XBOX GAME PASS GAMES

FORZA HORIZON 4

The fourth entry in this enduringly popular racing series is the best yet with a brand-new and expansive map of Great Britain to explore. There are masses of vehicles, events, and modes to enjoy, so there's plenty to keep you busy for a long time!

6

SONIC GENERATIONS

Fans have long debated whether 2-D or 3-D Sonic games are better. *Sonic Generations* offers the best of both, mixing the two styles in one of the hedgehog's top outings.

5

FAST FACT

As well as Xbox One games, you can also get Xbox 360 and original Xbox titles through Xbox Game Pass.

TEARAWAY UNFOLDED

This game, which takes place in a mesmerizing world made entirely out of paper, tasks you with using inventive and unique gameplay mechanics to make a special delivery.

4

3

SLY COOPER: THIEVES IN TIME

Travel around the world and through time in this stealth-based platformer. This entry has the sneaking and puzzling that fans know and love, but it also has cool unlockable costumes.

2

DiRT RALLY

Codemasters' rally game isn't for the faint of heart—it's tough to learn. Stick with it, though, and you'll discover an outstanding sports simulation that should satisfy all racing fans.

1

SEA OF THIEVES

Take to the seas via Xbox Game Pass in this brilliant pirate game from Rare. You'll need to work together with your shipmates to uncover as much treasure as you can get your hands on, but be careful, as other teams will be trying to do the same thing! Expect plenty of epic battles with other players along the way.

FAST FACT

PlayStation Now originally began as a streaming service, but these days, you can also download games to keep, as well as streaming titles, too.

FAST FACT

The music for *A Hat In Time* was co-composed by Scottish composer Grant Kirkhope, who also worked on the legendary *Banjo-Kazooie*.

A HAT IN TIME

TRAVEL THROUGH SPACE WITH HAT KID

Heroes don't come much cooler than a time-traveling girl wearing a top hat. In this colorful platformer you'll need to recover the fuel from Hat Kid's damaged ship. These Time Pieces have been scattered across a nearby planet and it's up to you to explore every corner of the world to gather your fuel and be on your way.

And that's just the main game. In the new DLC, there are more places to explore, extra enemies to fight, and new characters to meet. A new mission sees you exploring a huge cruise ship and helping the crew as you go. Elsewhere, a new mode challenges you with more difficult boss battles and stages. Clear them to unlock new options for your character.

QUICK TIPS!

SECRET ROOM
Use the Ice Hat on the pile of pillows in the bedroom and you'll access Hat Kid's secret hideout.

COMPLETIONIST
If you complete the game, head down to the lab connected to the basement to find a special hat.

DO A DANCE!
On your controller, press up, down, up, down on your directional pad. Your on-screen character will start to boogie!

TIME TO EXPLORE

HAT-TASTIC

There are six hats to collect in the game and each one grants you different powers. This top hat shows Hat Kid the way to the nearest point of interest, but she can wear hats that let her sprint, ground pound, and slow down time!

COLLECT-A-THON

With dozens of Time Pieces, badges, and relics to find across the game worlds, you'll need to look everywhere! The more you collect, the more abilities and areas you'll unlock. Don't stop till you've got them all.

STRANGE WORLDS

There are five locations to explore in the base game, with the additional cruise ship added in the free DLC. Each area is completely unique and themed to the particular location, so you'll always have somewhere new to explore.

JUMP FOR JOY

Every world holds unique challenges, enemies, and boss battles. You might be leaping over rings of energy or sprinting away from falling rocks to beat them. Between the big fights you'll find some fantastic platforming.

ALSO CHECK OUT . . .

SUPER MARIO ODYSSEY

This is without doubt the single best platformer of the current generation.

YOOKA-LAYLEE

A jumping chameleon partners with a flappy bat in this crazy platformer.

CUPHEAD

If you want a tough 2-D platforming challenge, this is perfect.

ULTIMATE RETRO COLLECTION

THE BEST CLASSIC GAMES YOU CAN PLAY TODAY!

Video games are always pushing forward, coming up with more impressive technology and surprising us with new ideas. But that doesn't mean new is always better. There are a host of classic retro games that can comfortably match the playability of games being released today. So if you want to experience some of the best games of all time and find out which titles influenced the games you're playing right now, then check out the legends on this list.

CRASH BANDICOOT
PS4

25

A classic 3-D platformer that's remembered fondly for its association with one of the greatest consoles of all time, the original PlayStation. Thanks to its re-release on PS4 as part of the *Crash Bandicoot N. Sane Trilogy*, it's easier to play than ever!

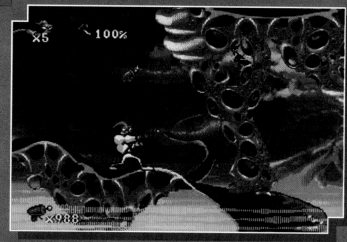

EARTHWORM JIM
STEAM, GOG

24

Earthworm Jim is a 16-bit comedy platformer full of crazy characters and slapstick fun. You play as a super suit–wearing earthworm— who became famous on the Genesis and SNES. The game is as humorous and fun as ever.

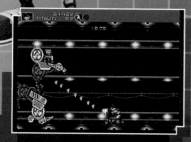

GUNSTAR HEROES
STEAM, PS4, XBOX ONE, SWITCH, iOS, ANDROID

23

This exciting, action-packed run 'n' gun game can be played alone, or with a co-op buddy. It's part of the *Sega Genesis Classics* collection. Progress through each level, blasting enemies on your way and then deal with the huge end of level bosses that you must defeat . . .

DONKEY KONG COUNTRY
VIRTUAL CONSOLE, NINTENDO 3DS, SUPER NES CLASSIC EDITION

22

Donkey Kong Country's graphics stunned the world when it was first released on the SNES back in 1994. It may not be state of the art now, but it still looks great and is full of cool ideas and fun levels.

PRINCE OF PERSIA: THE SANDS OF TIME
STEAM, GOG

21

All these years later, *Sands of Time* still feels fresh thanks to the clever way it uses a time-rewinding mechanic in combination with great 3-D platforming.

THEME HOSPITAL
ORIGIN, GOG

20 You take control of building and managing a hospital in this classic strategy game. It doesn't take itself too seriously but is still full of satisfying and in-depth strategic challenges that you can test yourself against.

FAST FACT

There are a total of 96 goals to find in *Super Mario World*. Some are easy and some require hunting for secret exits.

STREETS OF RAGE 2
STEAM, PS4, XBOX ONE, SWITCH, iOS, ANDROID

19 The enduring reputation of *Streets of Rage 2* as one of the best scrolling beat 'em ups ever made is enough to tell you why it's still worth playing today. You'll experience great music, cool moves, and some amazing retro-style pixel graphics.

SUPER MARIO BROS. 3
VIRTUAL CONSOLE, NES CLASSIC EDITION

18 Everyone knows that *Mario* platformers are great and every one of them is still worth playing. But for this list we've only focused on the very best, and *Super Mario 3* stands out.

REZ
PS4, STEAM, ANDROID

17 No one had seen anything like *Rez* when it was originally released on Dreamcast and PS2 in 2001 and no one has really made anything quite like it since. The musical rail shooter offers a hypnotizing experience that's been kept alive thanks to remakes—including a VR version.

CHRONO TRIGGER
STEAM, iOS, ANDROID, NINTENDO 3DS

16 In this epic RPG, you travel across time to defeat Lavos and save the world. Thanks to a great story, lovable characters, and a fantastic battle system, *Chrono Trigger* easily stands up to the high quality of RPGs being released today.

BEST RETRO CHARACTERS

MARIO

He's the most recognizable character in gaming and he's still appearing in incredible games today. One of his most recent, *Super Mario Odyssey*, is a fantastic 3-D platformer for the Nintendo Switch that gives Mario the ability to take over enemies by throwing his cap onto them.

SONIC

This super speedy blue hedgehog was once Mario's main rival in the 16-bit-era battle between Nintendo and Sega. He's since appeared alongside Mario in games like *Super Smash Bros.* and he's still appearing in his own video games, such as *Sonic Mania* and *Sonic Forces*.

DONKEY KONG

Donkey Kong's history goes all the way back to the *Donkey Kong* arcade game released in 1981, where Mario, then known as Jumpman, made his first appearance. *Donkey Kong* is still brawling in *Super Smash Bros.*, racing in *Mario Kart 8*, and platforming in his very own game, *Donkey Kong Country: Tropical Freeze*.

EEVEE

Eevee started off as just another Pokémon in the original game. However, the Pokémon's cute appearance and unique ability to evolve into different elemental versions made it popular with fans, to the point that Eevee has become a starter Pokémon in *Pokémon: Let's Go, Eevee!*

SAMUS

Players had made the mistake of assuming a man was inside Samus's power suit, but, in one of gaming's great moments, completing the first *Metroid* in under five hours would see her remove her helmet and reveal she was a woman. We can't wait to see her again in *Metroid Prime 4*.

THE SECRET OF MONKEY ISLAND
STEAM, GOG

15 This pirate-themed point-and-click adventure is one of the most influential games of all time. You won't regret checking out where this legendary adventure series started.

LEMMINGS
PLAYSTATION VITA, iOS, ANDROID

14 At the start of every level, your lemmings will start walking toward danger. By equipping lemmings with special skills to help them avoid that danger, you must try to save as many of the cute creatures as possible.

TETRIS
PS4, iOS, ANDROID

13 *Tetris* has been released in many forms since it took the world by storm on the Game Boy in 1989. The truth is, whichever version you play, whether it's the mobile re-releases, or the recent *Tetris Effect*, featuring awesome music and VR support, you'll still be enjoying the same special shape-slotting puzzling that's made every version of this game great.

SONIC THE HEDGEHOG 2
STEAM, PS4, XBOX ONE, SWITCH, iOS, ANDROID

12 Despite all the *Sonic* games released over the years, few have come close to the glory of this speedy Sega Genesis classic. This is Sonic at his best.

SIMCITY 2000
ORIGIN, GOG

11 The city building management series *SimCity* is still going strong today, but many still consider 1993's *SimCity 2000* to be the entry that struck the best balance between accessibility and deep gameplay.

SUPER METROID
VIRTUAL CONSOLE, SUPER NES CLASSIC EDITION

9 *Super Metroid* is such an influential game that its name was used—along with *Castlevania*—to name a genre: Metroidvanias. By exploring the game's world, you find new power-ups—such as the Morphing Ball and Grappling Beam—to help you access some cool new areas.

STREET FIGHTER II
PS4, XBOX ONE, SWITCH, STEAM

10 There's hardly a platform that exists that doesn't have some sort of version of *Street Fighter II* on it. That tells you just how good the game that defined the fighting genre is and how much fun it still is to play.

FAST FACT

Grim Fandango Remastered was released by Double Fine, the studio owned by Tim Schafer, the game's original writer.

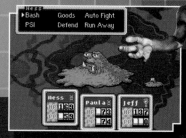

EARTHBOUND
VIRTUAL CONSOLE, SUPER NES CLASSIC EDITION

8 *EarthBound*'s sense of fun, along with its classic turn-based battling, have made it one of the most beloved RPGs of all time and earned it "must-play" status.

ODDWORLD: ABE'S ODDYSEE
STEAM, GOG, PS4, XBOX ONE, iOS, ANDROID

7 This classic puzzle platformer has a star character full of personality, an amazing-looking world, a great sense of humor, and brilliant puzzles. Both the original version and a faithful remake are easily available, offering two great ways to experience it.

GRIM FANDANGO
STEAM, GOG, PS4, XBOX ONE, SWITCH, iOS, ANDROID

6 Thanks to its recent re-release in the form of a remastered edition, it's as easy as ever to play this legendary adventure game about a skeleton called Manny and his epic journey across the Land of the Dead.

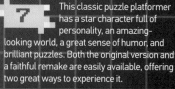

MODERN RETRO CLASSICS
COOL NEW GAMES INSPIRED BY THE PAST

SONIC MANIA

Sonic Mania includes remixed versions of classic levels from *Sonic* games of the past, as well as brand-new stages faithful to the 2-D pixel look and gameplay style of the first few entries in the *Sonic* series. It's one of the best *Sonic* games ever made.

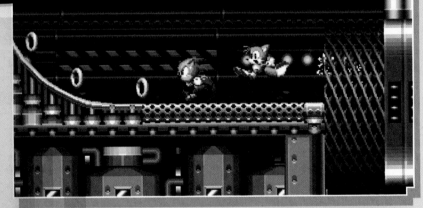

STARDEW VALLEY

After being left unsatisfied by modern entries in the *Harvest Moon* series, the developer behind *Stardew Valley* decided to create his own version of the classic. The result is an amazing pixel art farming sim that also includes exploration, combat, and a town.

UNDERTALE

One look at *Undertale*'s old-school graphics and you can tell that it's a retro-inspired video game. To be precise, the game draws elements from the *Mother* series—also known as *EarthBound*—the *Mario & Luigi* role-playing games, and the *Touhou Project* bullet hell shooter.

THE MESSENGER

A side-scrolling action-platformer where you play as a ninja. Visuals take inspiration from two eras of retro gaming. It's set during two periods: The past uses 8-bit-style graphics and sound, while the future uses 16-bit.

OCTOPATH TRAVELER

Square Enix's attempt to return to the roots of its classic RPGs, such as the *Final Fantasy* series. It uses an old-school turn-based battle system and a visual style the developers call "HD-2-D," referring to a mix of 16-bit-style SNES graphics with modern HD effects.

SHADOW OF THE COLOSSUS
PS4

5 Originally released on the PlayStation 2, *Shadow of the Colossus* is a game in which you must take down huge, building-sized bosses that have to be climbed to be beaten. It received a re-release on PS3 and, more recently, a remake on PS4.

DAY OF THE TENTACLE
STEAM, GOG, PS4, IOS

4 Another classic adventure that's been blessed with the remaster treatment, *Day of the Tentacle* is a hilarious time-traveling point-and-click where you play as three characters stuck in the present, past, and future. The remastered version offers you the choice to play with the beautiful pixel art of the original.

THE LEGEND OF ZELDA: OCARINA OF TIME
NINTENDO 3DS

3 This game is always near the top of "greatest games of all time" lists thanks to the influence it's had on gaming, as well as how much fun it is to play today. Link's first 3-D adventure is still one of his best.

FAST FACT

The creator of the *Pokémon* series, Satoshi Tajiri, got the idea for the game from his childhood hobby of insect collecting.

POKÉMON RED AND BLUE
VIRTUAL CONSOLE, SWITCH

2 The original *Pokémon* game is still one of the best, introducing us to some of the series' favorite Pokémon, including the lovable Pikachu. You can play the original version via Virtual Console on 3DS or enjoy the recent Switch remake, *Pokémon: Let's Go, Pikachu!* and *Pokémon: Let's Go, Eevee!*

SUPER MARIO WORLD
VIRTUAL CONSOLE, SUPER NES CLASSIC EDITION

1 It's not only the greatest *Mario* game of all time, the greatest platformer of all time, or even the greatest retro game ever made. Some still say that *Super Mario World* is simply the best video game ever. Whether it really is *the* best or just one of the best doesn't really matter. What matters is that its classic levels, cool power-ups, and pixel-perfect platforming is still fantastic fun. Ever wondered why Mario is such a gaming legend? Then play this.

FAST FACT

You get your first weapon from the village elder who says, "It's dangerous to go alone!" A homage to the NES classic *The Legend of Zelda*.

MOONLIGHTER

DUNGEON SHOPKEEPER

By day, you're running a humble little shop in the village of Rynoka, trading in goods to adventurers or people just looking for a bargain. But by night, you're setting off into the nearby mysterious dungeons scouring for loot that you can sell back to your customers the next day. Take as much rare loot as your backpack and pockets can carry. Take your profits to invest in better gear so that you're ready to face even more dangers and find even more precious treasures.

But there's something strange about these dungeons. The layouts change each time, while formidable bosses await deep inside. Have you got what it takes for this risky venture? Can you make this adventure pay off?

QUICK TIPS!

HEALING POOLS
Dungeon layouts aren't completely random. If you find a healing pool, you're usually heading in the right direction. Plus, you can heal!

GROWING THE COMMUNITY
Be sure to invest in the community, such as the apothecary or blacksmith. Their services will help you in return.

WISH LIST
Crafting better gear requires the right materials. Use the wish list to keep track so you don't accidentally sell 'em!

BEST BUSINESS PRACTICES 101

HOW MUCH?

When you first put your loot up for sale, you don't know what they're actually worth. You're free to set the prices and see how a customer reacts. You're allowed to keep tweaking the prices until you hit a sweet spot.

THE CUSTOMER IS ALWAYS RIGHT, RIGHT?

You might want to get a sale, but if a customer's emoticon is flashing with coins in their eyes, it means they've found a huge bargain—which means you're underselling yourself. Remember: You want to maximize your profits!

REQUESTS AND SUSPICIOUS CUSTOMERS

Some customers will come in looking for specific artifacts or perhaps even weapons and they'll pay you handsomely. But as you get more successful, watch out for thieves looking for a five-finger discount. Tackle them with a roll!

SHOP EXPANSION

You can also invest in upgrades, eventually turning your humble shop into a lavish emporium with special displays for the rarest items. Or why not simply upgrade your cash register to get more tips? Cha-ching!

ALSO CHECK OUT ...

DEAD CELLS
A deadly, action-packed roguelite with all sorts of lovely loot!

HYPER LIGHT DRIFTER
Beautiful pixel art combined with some challenging top-down action.

CRYPT OF THE NECRODANCER
Survive this roguelite with the power of rhythm!

GLOSSARY

4K
Ultra-high-definition resolution, supported by high-end TVs and monitors. The actual resolution is 3840 x 2160, boasting four times as many pixels as a 1080p display.

AI
"Artificial intelligence," the code used to make in-game characters behave as they do. *The Last Guardian* is a great example of complex AI, used to make Trico behave like a real creature, but it's also what powers enemies in nearly every game.

AR
Augmented reality; a fusion of the real world and digital assets. *Pokémon GO* uses this to great effect by superimposing wild Pokémon over a live feed from your phone's camera, and various Vita and 3DS games also embrace this new technology.

Battle royale
A genre that combines last-one-standing gameplay with survival and exploration elements. Best demonstrated in *Fortnite Battle Royale* and *Apex Legends*.

Beta
A game in an unfinished state, sometimes with select players (a "closed beta") or the public at large (an "open beta") invited to test key features ahead of release. Occasionally, developers will offer this access even earlier—this is known as the "alpha" phase.

Boss
A bigger, badder enemy commonly seen at the end of a level or guarding something particularly valuable. These larger foes tend to test all of your gaming skills and come with amazing rewards if you're able to beat them.

Bug
An error in a game that causes something unexpected to happen. May also be referred to as a glitch, depending on the nature of the bug. Some are extremely minor—such as several objects clipping into one another—while the most harmful can completely prevent progress. Save often, just in case!

Camping
The act of hanging around in one spot in a multiplayer game, usually either near where enemies spawn into a map or in a remote area, using a long-range weapon to repeatedly pick off players. Camping is usually frowned upon by rivals.

Casting
Can be short for either "broadcasting"—using services like Twitch, Beam, and YouTube to stream live gameplay—or "shoutcasting," which is play-by-play commentary of a gaming event, much like with live sports on TV.

CCG
"Collectible card game," although you may also see TCG, which is "trading card game." They're effectively the same thing, though—games like *Hearthstone* where you earn new cards to make the very best deck you can.

Clutch
An unlikely comeback against all the odds is known as a clutch play. A good example would be using your Ultimate as the last hero standing to wipe out the enemy team, and prevent the payload from being delivered in the dying seconds of an *Overwatch* game.

Co-op
Teaming up with other players to work together toward a common goal. Co-op games usually increase the difficulty based on the number of players, so bear that in mind if you don't feel like your group is up to the challenge!

Cosplay
The art of creating costumes based on video-game characters and often wearing them to events and conventions. Cosplay isn't limited to video games—enthusiasts also cosplay as movie, comic book, and anime characters as well!

Cross-up
An attack that forces the opponent to block from the opposite direction in a fighting game, usually performed by jumping over them to clip them in the back of the head. Some characters can perform cross-ups by dashing or teleporting through opponents as well.

DLC

Downloadable content. Extra levels, maps, characters, outfits, items, and modes made available for a game after release are collectively known as DLC.

DPS

"Damage per second," which can either refer to how much damage a character or weapon is able to do, or even characters whose role is primarily to deal damage, such as Black Mages in *Final Fantasy XIV* or Tracer in *Overwatch*.

Easter egg

A secret hidden in a game that typically serves no function other than to amuse or entertain. These can sometimes be references to other games or even other media entirely.

Esports

Professional gaming, as played by both individuals and full teams depending on the game being played. Prize pools are often massive for the biggest events, and the standard of play is incredibly high—major events are even broadcast live, just like a real sporting event.

F2P

"Free-To-Play," referring to games that can be downloaded and played for free. These often have some kind of in-game purchases, so watch out for those, but remember: Never spend anything without getting your parents' permission!

FPS

First-person shooter—a game genre where you see through the eyes of the character, like *Destiny 2* or *Apex Legends*.

Frame rate

The number of individual images that make up one second of moving game visuals. Thirty frames per second (30fps) is common, and offers relatively smooth performance, with higher frame rates looking even smoother.

GG

"Good game." This is used in chat after multiplayer games in order to congratulate everyone involved on their success.

Griefing

Doing something just to annoy other players in a multiplayer game. This can be anything from standing in a doorway, so people can't get through, to attacking your own teammates. Don't do this—play nice!

Grinding

Repeating the same actions over and over again, like running in circles in tall grass in *Pokémon* to raise your team's levels, or doing the same quest repeatedly in *Monster Hunter* in the hopes of getting a rare reward.

HDR

A relatively new term, HDR stands for "high dynamic range," and is something you only see in new, high-end displays and TVs. Supported games boast much brighter and more vibrant colors in HDR than on a standard set—*Rez*'s Area X is one mind-blowing example.

Indie

"Independent"; refers to games or studios that don't have support from a major publisher. Indie studios are typically quite small, but the games that they create are often incredibly creative and original.

Kiting

The act of manipulating enemy placement to your advantage, such as a tank pulling a boss away from other players in an MMO, or Link running circles around enemies that only have close-range attacks.

Lag

A delay between player inputs and on-screen actions, usually caused by poor connections in online games. Minor lag is generally bearable, but extreme cases can make games unplayable.

Leaderboard

A high-score table. These are usually online elements, so you can see how your best results compare against the world's greatest players!

Metroidvania

A genre where exploration and back-tracking are key features,

using new abilities that are unlocked to allow you to open previously inaccessible areas. *Hollow Knight* is one such example.

Mid-laner
A player who stays in the central area in MOBAs like *Dota 2*. There are also top- and bottom-laners.

MMO
"Massively multiplayer online"; games where many players can connect and communicate with one another. Most common are RPGs, but some—like *Sea of Thieves*—tackle other genres as well.

MOBA
"Multiplayer online battle arena" describes online games such as *League of Legends* and *Dota 2*. It's a relatively new genre, but one of the most popular in the world today!

Mod
Additional software that can alter how a game looks or plays, or even add completely new features. Though most common on PC, these are starting to be seen on consoles as well.

Noob
This is short for "newbie," a term used to describe someone who is new to playing a particular game. However, it is more commonly heard as an insult used against bad players.

NPC
NPC—or non-playable character—is the term used to refer to a non-hostile character. They might be important, like a quest-giver, or they might just be someone who exists in the game world.

Permadeath
Refers to games where progress is lost upon death, forcing players to start over from scratch. Titles such as *Nuclear Throne* and *Don't Starve* are good examples of this.

Port
A game that is adapted from one system to another, sometimes with improvements (if the new system is more powerful than the original), or cuts to get it running on a weaker platform.

Patch
A post-release update for a game that fixes bugs and/or adds new content. These are growing increasingly common.

Post-game
Not all games end when the credits roll—in some cases, that's when the real fun begins! Games like *Pokémon* are rich in post-game content, and there's loads you can do after the game is "over."

PvE
"Player Versus Environment," a term used to refer to modes in games (typically ones with multiplayer components) where players take on AI opponents together rather than competing against one another.

PvP
The opposite of PvE, this stands for "Player Versus Player," meaning competitive multiplayer modes rather than co-operative ones.

Reboot
A game that looks to reinvent a series while returning to its roots, usually reverting to a basic title rather than using numbers or subtitles.

Remaster
This is a little different than a full remake—remasters tend to be slight upgrades of older games for new systems, using the same characters and levels, often sporting enhanced graphics or new modes.

Re-spec
Being able to cancel and redo things like skill-point distribution or other stats, enabling you to deal with various situations by quickly changing a character's specializations in a matter of seconds. A very useful feature!

Rogue-like
A genre of games where procedural generation is used to make every dungeon, session, or adventure different. It's named after classic 1980 dungeon-crawler *Rogue*.

RPG
"Role-playing game," sometimes encountered with additional letters: JRPG refers to Japanese titles, ARPG is used for action-heavy RPGs, MMORPG means online games, while SRPG means "strategy RPG," describing games such as *Fire Emblem*.

RTS
"Real-time strategy," a genre that shot to popularity with games like *Command & Conquer* and *StarCraft*, now dominated by the likes of the *Total War* series.

Sandbox
Open-world games where players are free to play around and experiment however they wish—things like the Hub areas in LEGO games or the open worlds of *Minecraft* and *Dragon Quest Builders*.

Scrub
An insult aimed at bad players, or those who rely on cheap, basic tactics, such as spamming the same moves over and over in a fighting game.

Sherpa
A player who helps others through difficult content in multiplayer games, such as Raids in *Destiny 2*. Sherpas are usually experts who know their way around, and often there's little in it for them outside of just being helpful.

Season Pass
Modern games often have downloadable extras that offer the ability to pre-purchase all of it in one bundle—this kind of package is known as a season pass, but actual contents will vary from game to game.

Speedrun
The act of playing through games as quickly as possible, often using glitches and other tricks to beat games in record time. Runners often post their best efforts online, and compete with others on ranking sites to see who is the fastest at any given game.

Tank
A strong character in a game whose job is to soak up damage and protect more fragile characters. Tanks are common in MMO games, but you'll also find them in class-based online games like *Overwatch*.

Top-deck
In a card game, top-decking is where you find yourself relying on the next card you draw, whether it's because your hand is empty or because you find yourself in a situation where there are only a couple of cards in your deck that will actually be useful.

Trolling
Misbehaving in an online game purely to annoy other players. This comes in many forms, from getting in the way of others, or hurting your own team, to intentionally doing the opposite of what you're supposed to do. Don't do it!

UGC
"User-generated content"; describes things that players have made using in-game tools. Original *Minecraft* worlds and *Roblox* games are all perfect examples of this.

Vanilla
Used to refer to the original version of a game before patches and updates are applied. Vanilla base games are sometimes still supported, but in other cases, the only way to play the original versions is on special fan-run servers.

VR
Virtual reality, the hot new technology that is taking the gaming world by storm. Players wear headsets and are completely immersed in the action, moving as if it's really happening around them.

Whiff
To miss with an attack or move. This can either be completely accidental or done intentionally to mess with other players, or for some other purpose, like building meter in fighting games.

XP
"Experience points"; used to level up in RPGs or any progress system like those of the *Forza* games. Sometimes written as EXP, but the purpose is typically the same—gain loads and level up!